DAMN THE DISABILITIES

DAMN THE DISABILITIES:
FULL SPEED AHEAD

Young Athletes Who Would Not
Be Defeated!

JACK CAVANAUGH

WRS
PUBLISHING

A Division of WRS Group, Inc.
Waco, Texas

First published in the United States of America in 1995 by WRS Publishing, A Division of WRS Group, Inc., 701 N. New Road, Waco, Texas 76710
Book design by Colleen Robishaw, Yvonne Chiu
Jacket design by Joe James
Jacket photo by Stephen Castagneto

10 9 8 7 6 5 4 3 2 1

Library of Congress Cataloging-in-Publication Data

Cavanaugh, Jack.
    Damn the Disabilities : full speed ahead : young athletes who
would not be defeated! / Jack Cavanaugh.
        p.   cm.
    ISBN 1-56796-057-X : $13.95
    1. Athletes--United States--Biography. 2. Physically handicapped-
-United States--Biography.   I. Title.
GV697.A1C34   1995
796'.087'0922--dc20
    [B]   94-29917
                                                                CIP

DEDICATION

To my wife, Marge,
and my children, John and Tara.

And also to everyone, athlete or not,
who has refused to let a disability or handicap
deter them from living
as full a life as possible.

TABLE of CONTENTS

ACKNOWLEDGMENTS

Putting together a book that focuses on so many distinctly different individuals is a daunting task. Compiling one that involves a collection of remarkable people who overcame severe disabilities or handicaps to excel in sports—in some cases after barely surviving horrifying accidents—is also an extraordinary emotional experience, albeit a rewarding one.

Apart from the cooperation of the athletes themselves, along with dancer Dawn Storrs and baseball announcer Don Wardlow, I was aided immeasurably by their families in what, for many of them, meant reliving nearly tragic or, at least, sorrowful times in their lives. Without exception, family members and friends that I interviewed were extremely cooperative, no doubt because of their pride in what their son, daughter, or friend had accomplished in the face of extreme adversity.

For many, recounting the events surrounding near-fatal accidents or other personal calamities or serious misfortunes were painful experiences, often done haltingly and with tears and, always, with great emotion. Never, in a long writing and reporting career, have I ever been so deeply moved by so many remarkable and inspirational stories.

Among those owed thanks for their assistance in this project are National Handicapped Sports, the U.S. Association for Blind Athletes, the Springfield, Massachusetts, unit of the Shriners Hospitals for Crippled Children, the National Foundation of Wheelchair Tennis, the U.S. Blind Athletes Association National Goalball Team, the Newington (Connecticut) Children's Hospital, the New Britain (Connecticut) Red Sox baseball club, the Professional Golfers' Association of America, and the U.S. Disabled Sports Team.

A note of gratitude is also due Brian Zevnik, my agent, who believed in this project from the start and provided encouragement along the way.

INTRODUCTION

It never occurred to Chris Samele that he might never play basketball again—not even as he lay on a snow-covered embankment staring at his left leg which had just been severed in a car accident two days before Christmas in 1988. But he did, playing three seasons at Torrington High School in Connecticut as one of the team's best outside shooters who, despite an artificial left leg, also drove to the basket often.

Similarly, Larry Alford, rather than being overwhelmed with depression and self-pity after losing the lower part of his left arm in a highway crash, became more determined than ever to make it on the Professional Golfers' Association (PGA) tour. Less than a year after his accident, Larry, then eighteen and wearing a specially designed prosthesis where his left arm had been, broke eighty during one of his first golf outings since he was critically injured.

Likewise, the gradual loss of sight did not deter Jeni Armbruster from continuing to play basketball, even when she no longer could see the basket, her teammates, or her opponents, and could barely make out the outline of the backboard. Despite her adversity, Jeni remained a deadly outside shooter for her high school team in Colorado Springs before becoming totally blind and developing into one of the best goalball players in the world.

In an era of pampered and overpaid professional athletes who beg off from playing while nursing the slightest of injuries, Samele, Alford, and Armbruster epitomize young amateurs who play their sports with a passion despite seemingly insuperable physical handicaps, and play them well. There are others, many others—more and more each year—who continue to excel in sports, the most noteworthy being Jim Abbott, the big league pitcher who was born without a right hand. As a boy Abbott had been inspired by another ballplayer, Pete Gray, a one-armed outfielder who spent the 1945 season with the old St. Louis Browns followed by a spectacular minor league and semipro career.

Watching Gray perform wondrous feats in the outfield with one arm and hit .218—a fairly respectable average in the 1990s for some million-dollar-a-year big leaguers—many fans were moved to wonder how much better Gray might have been with two arms. But Gray said he might not have been as good. "If I'd had two arms, I probably wouldn't have tried so hard to succeed," he told me once in his hometown of Nanticoke, Pennsylvania.

Tried so hard. That was a recurring theme uttered by most of the athletes and the others, including a dancer and a blind baseball announcer, whose inspiring stories are recounted in this book—how they put an inordinate amount of effort into their sports, trying so hard to succeed and, in sports, often against able-bodied athletes. Their stories are a testament to the human spirit—incredible triumphs over physical adversity which helped raise their self-esteem and enabled them to compete, some amazingly well, to play the games they loved with a passion.

My first encounter with a handicapped athlete was in a pickup basketball game at the West Side Y.M.C.A. in New York in the early 1970s. One of the players was a young man, perhaps in his late twenties, whose right arm ended at the elbow, forcing him to do everything with his left arm— pass the ball, catch it, dribble, and shoot. He did it all with remarkable dexterity. Most of the other players in the game were "regulars" at this particular Y; I was not. It was obvious that they just accepted him as another player, and a very good one at that, but I myself could not help but be fascinated. Not long after, I came upon a brief reference to Pete Gray in a sports book, that related how after catching a ball, he would throw it to an infielder or to home plate with the same arm, the only one he had. Though Gray had been highly publicized when the Browns brought him up to the big leagues during the World War II war year of 1945, I knew little about him and realized that many people had probably never even heard of Pete Gray.

This gave me an idea for a magazine story that I wrote in the 1970s after tracking down Gray. This was not an easy task, since he led a reclusive life after leaving baseball in the 1950s. For example, he had no phone and rarely granted interviews. Fortunately for me, Gray was Lithuanian (the family name was Wyshner) and coming from a Lithuanian family myself, I could speak a little Lithuanian and did, at the very outset, when I finally found Pete. It broke the ice and we seemed to hit it off somehow, and I stayed in touch with him for years. Pete was never very communicative, to say the least, even if you did speak Lithuanian. But talking to him, and later to some of his friends and former big league teammates, I became fascinated with the man who had spent most of his time since his retirement from baseball playing golf—scoring in the eighties, and sometimes in the seventies—usually for money; hustling pool players in Scranton and Wilkes-Barre, not far from Nanticoke, where he lived all of his life; and playing cards, also for money.

This fascination with the old "One-Armed-Wonder," as he was called by some sportswriters in the 1940s and 1950s, led to an interest in handicapped athletes in general. Thereafter, whenever I saw a story in a newspaper or magazine about a handicapped athlete, I would clip it out and file it. Friends, aware of my interest in disabled athletes were also helpful, often informing me of television segments they had seen about people like David Potter of Houston. Although Potter has no hands, he played Little League baseball while wearing a special "scoop" throwing and catching "arm" which had been designed for him by a new teammate, Josh Parsons. Apart from Gray, former N.F.L. star Pat Summerall (now a well-known sports broadcaster) and a few others, this book deals mainly with young athletes who were still competing when I wrote it in 1994.

Among those you will meet in these pages are Jonathan Slifka who, though confined to a wheelchair, played Little League baseball batting over .300 one season (a teammate ran for him) and playing second base. A good wheelchair tennis player, Slifka at first failed to make his high school tennis team, one of the best in Connecticut. But the coach at Hall High School in West Hartford was so impressed with Jonathan that he asked him if he would agree to warm up Hall players before their home games and to chart opponents. He did, for one season in 1992, and then the following year, determined to play himself, made and played for the Hall junior varsity, competing against able-bodied players.

Then there is Dawn Storrs, a highly promising dancer, who at the age of sixteen was involved in an auto accident that essentially severed her right leg. Hearing surgeons in a

hospital emergency room discuss amputation of the leg—
which was held together in the back by a thread of muscle
tissue—she screamed out, "Please don't amputate my leg!
You have to save it! If you amputate it, I'll die, because I'm
a dancer, and I can't live without dancing." Surgeons saved
the leg, and less than a year later, Dawn Storrs began a
remarkable comeback.

Perhaps the most surprising thing about all of these
people—a common thread that runs through all of them—
is their lack of self-pity and their resolute determination to
succeed in their sport (in Dawn Storrs' case, as a dancer)
despite their disabilities and to be accepted as athletes and
not patronized. Each one is a profile in courage and an
inspiration to other young athletes who have refused to let
their disabilities deter them from playing their favorite sport,
be it in the Paralympics, the Special Olympics, or the
Challenger Division of the Little League for physically and
mentally handicapped youngsters.

Far more than whining millionaire athletes, they
exemplify the best in their sports, imbuing them with a
special kind of beauty and purity, and clearly demonstrating
that competing, not winning, is everything.

DAMN THE DISABILITIES

CHAPTER 1

CHRIS SAMELE

Chris Samele felt on top of the world. At the age of fifteen, he was fast becoming a basketball legend in his hometown of Torrington, Connecticut, after leading St. Peter's to the state parochial grammar school championship the previous season as an eighth-grader with a remarkable 41-point scoring average. No one doubted that he would become a star in high school and then go on to an outstanding collegiate career. While a freshman at Torrington High, he had already scored 50 points in two junior varsity games, and on December 23, 1988, he was scheduled to play in his third.

It was early afternoon, and a combination of light snow and sleet was falling as Chris rode in a car with friends. They were bound for Waterbury to do some last-minute Christmas shopping after classes had been dismissed early to start the Christmas vacation. In the car with young Samele (pronounced SUH-MEEL) were two other Torrington High boy athletes and three girl cheerleaders, one of whom was driving. Laughter engulfed the car as it sped along Route 8 through the quiet northwestern Connecticut countryside.

Suddenly in Thomaston, about midway between Torrington and Waterbury, the car hit an icy patch and careened wildly out of control. The laughter inside turned to panic as the car spun around several times, then bounced off a guard rail on the right side of the two-lane southbound section of the highway. When the car hit the guard rail, the impact blew out the rear window. In seconds, three of the four teenagers sitting in the back, including Chris Samele, were sucked through the hole and catapulted onto the roadway. Meantime, the sixteen-year-old driver finally brought the car to a halt.

Amid the tranquil tableau of fresh-fallen snow on the surrounding hillside, the scene on the highway was one of horror. The first of the two cheerleaders hurtled through the blown-out window, Shawn Collins, lay dead about fifty feet in front of the car. About twenty-five feet behind her body, Chris Samele, dazed but conscious, struggled to sit up. In front of him, about twenty feet away, Samele spotted the truncated part of his leg, which had been severed above the knee. "I thought the whole thing was a dream," Chris recalled more than five years later. "The first thing I thought of was my basketball—the fact that we had a game that very night—and whether I could ever play again."

Lying alongside him, within touching distance, was the other cheerleader who had been flung through the rear window and critically injured. For Chris, the pain was excruciating; yet the sight of his severed leg was practically overwhelming. Even the sight of the blood surging from his wound did not faze him, nor did the possibility that he might be in a life-threatening situation. Incredulous, he continued to stare at what had been his left leg.

Meanwhile, stunned by the tragedy, but uninjured, the driver and the other two boys got out of the car—which was undamaged except for the blown-out rear window— and hurried to the sides of their friends. "Chris, Chris, just try to take it easy," said one of his basketball teammates and longtime friends, Brian Anzellotti, while kneeling at his side. "Everything's going to be all right. Help will be here any minute."

Looking at his teammate, young Samele pointed to his left leg and said, "But Brian, look at my leg. How am I going to play ball again?"

Cars on both sides of the highway began to slow down. The first to stop was a pickup truck carrying two brothers from Thomaston, Jack and Tom Watson, then twenty-three and twenty-one years old. "When we saw how profusely the blood was gushing from Chris's stump, we got a rope from the truck and used it to apply pressure to the leg to stop the flow of blood," Jack Watson said. "Then we folded the left leg of his sweat pants under the stump. As we were working on Chris, he looked up and said, 'I'm never going to play basketball again. And I have to play.' I said to him, 'We have your leg and we're going to have them take it to the hospital and reattach it. You'll be able to play basketball again.' Of course I didn't know if the doctors could do it, but I just wanted to comfort Chris a bit. Then we wrapped the severed part of his leg in a blanket and propped it under the stump while waiting for the ambulances to arrive. Chris watched without saying a word."

Linda Samele was in the kitchen of her white Cape Cod-style home on Bird Street in Torrington, an old industrial city twenty miles northwest of Waterbury. A wreath adorned the front door, and for the first time ever, a live Christmas tree, rather than the customary artificial one, stood fully decorated in the living room. With Christmas only two days away and her son encouraged by his good start on the junior varsity basketball team, Mrs. Samele could hardly have been happier as she prepared a homemade sauce for the homemade manicotti the family would have for dinner before leaving for Chris's game that evening against Wilby High. Downstairs in the family room, her husband, Bob, a Torrington mailman, watched television. Nearby were more than fifty trophies his son had won playing basketball, some of them on teams that Bob Samele had coached. Photos of young Chris, both in basketball and baseball uniforms from the time he was seven, were displayed prominently in the room.

It was 1:40 P.M., Linda Samele recalls, when the phone call came from Waterbury Hospital. She was told there had been accident, and her son had been hurt, but, the caller added, he was conscious and talking. Could she and her husband get to the hospital as soon as possible? In minutes, Linda and Bob Samele were driving along Route 8, bound for Waterbury Hospital. The snow and sleet had stopped, it had gotten warmer and the ice on the highway had turned to slush. On the way, they came upon what was obviously an accident scene. Seeing a white car they believed belonged to one of Chris's teammates, they assumed it was the one their only child was in when he had been hurt. "I noticed that the back window was out, but otherwise the car was not damaged," Linda Samele said. "So Bob and I assumed it had been a minor accident. We then breathed a sigh of relief as we continued on to the hospital."

At the hospital, the Sameles were escorted into a room off the waiting room and, with a priest and social worker present, were told by two doctors what had happened. "We looked at each other and became hysterical," remembered Linda, a teacher's aide in a Torrington elementary school. "One of the doctors said that when they brought Chris into the emergency room he was in great pain but was unbelievably calm and completely composed. 'You would have been proud of him,' he told us." *And I thought to myself, we always have been.*

As the day and night wore on, a remarkable scene began to unfold in the hospital waiting room. By 7:00 P.M., about seventy people—family members, friends, teachers, coaches, and the principal of Torrington High School—had gathered there after having heard of Chris Samele's accident. (Dawn Storrs, the seriously injured cheerleader, was taken to St. Mary's Hospital, also in Waterbury so that there would be sufficient surgeons available to perform surgery on both of them simultaneously.) Among the group was Rob Martin, a guidance counselor at the high school who was also the boys' varsity basketball coach.

Chris Samele underwent surgery for almost seven hours. Finally, at about 9:00 P.M. after an agonizing wait spent mainly with family members, his parents were told they could see their son. "I went in first with the minister from my church," recalled Linda Samele, who is a Lutheran (her husband is a Roman Catholic). "My heart was pounding and I was a nervous wreck.

"We hugged each other. Then Chris looked up at me and said, 'Mommy, you are going to get me a new leg, aren't you? I'll play basketball again, I know I will.' Then Bob came into the room and, as they hugged each other, Chris said, 'Dad, I lost my leg.' And Bob said, 'I know, but you're going to get better. There's a big group of people down in the waiting room, including Coach Martin, who are praying for you right now.'"

At the mention of the coach's name, Chris Samele's face brightened. "You mean Coach Martin is there, too?" he asked. "Tell him, I'll be out this year, but that I'll be back next season. I'm going to play basketball again. I've come too far to stop now."

Because of the accident, Torrington's game against Wilby High that night was called off. Torrington is a red-hot basketball town. But on this sad night, people in Torrington were not thinking basketball, or even Christmas; they were thinking about, and praying for Shawn Collins, Dawn Storrs, and Chris Samele.

From the time their son was very young, Linda and Bob Samele knew that Chris was something special, and not just as an athlete. "He was always very sensitive towards others," Linda recounted. "When he was in nursery school, a boy named Steven Jausch broke his leg. After that, the other kids stayed away from him because, with the cast on and unable to play, he was considered 'different.' But Chris went out of his way to help him. He'd carry the Jausch boy's books and do other things for him until he got better.

"Another time we were on the beach at Point Judith, Rhode Island, and Chris was playing with another little boy. When we were leaving, Bob and I asked Chris where his matchbox toys were and he told us the other boy liked them so much that he gave them to him. But it didn't surprise us. And he was always concerned about relatives. For instance, if my sister came for a visit, after she left to drive home, Chris would say to Bob or to me, 'Why don't you call Auntie Mame to make sure she got home all right.' After we did, you could see he was relieved, even as a little kid."

From the start, Bob Samele says his son was a remarkably determined athlete. "When he was six, I put a basket on our garage and he would be out in the driveway shooting and practicing his dribbling for hours, no matter how cold it was, and sometimes even when it was snowing," his father recalled. "Gradually as he got bigger, I would raise the basket, and he got better and better. He was always much better than the other kids his age, but he never hogged the ball and was always concerned about his teammates getting their shots. He was a good baseball player, too, and, when he was thirteen, he was voted rookie of the year in the Torrington Babe Ruth League. But even after a baseball game, he often would to out in the driveway and shoot."

By the time he was thirteen, Chris Samele's basketball exploits as a junior player had attracted attention outside of Torrington. After he had led St. Peter's to the state championship, coaches from several prep schools in Connecticut approached the Sameles and offered Chris scholarships. "But Chris wanted to go to high school in Torrington with his friends," Bob ·Samele said. "And back then he wanted to go to Notre Dame. I remember him telling me when he was in the eighth grade, 'Don't worry about tuition, Dad. I'll get a free ride [a scholarship] to Notre Dame.'"

Coach Rob Martin knew all about Chris Samele when he got to Torrington High. "I'd seen him play when he was in the seventh and eighth grades, and you could tell he was going to be a tremendous player," Martin said. "But even though he was already an outstanding player, I wanted to bring him along slowly on the freshman and J.V. teams. There was no doubt in my mind that he was going to be one of the best high school players in the state. And he was, and still is, a great kid."

At Waterbury Hospital, Chris Samele underwent five operations on his leg in seven days. But never once during his three-and-a-half-week hospital stay did he ever show any signs of depression or self-pity. "It was amazing. When we went to see Chris at first, we'd feel terrible," Linda Samele said. "But then we'd walk into his room and he'd be shooting baskets with a Nerf ball and a hoop that the father of a teammate had brought him. And he'd be smiling and in good spirits. He'd make us laugh, and we always felt so much better when we left. It was the same with friends and relatives. They'd tell us how they'd be crying on the way to the hospital, feeling so sorry for Chris. And then he would tell them not to feel sorry for him because he was doing just fine. And they'd eventually leave laughing, with their spirits raised. But that's they way he's always been—good-natured, never complaining about anything. We think we brought him up right, taught him proper values and so on. But we can't take all the credit for raising such a great kid." But Chris Samele, asked to explain how he turned out the way he did—sensitive of others, uncomplaining, and fiercely determined—says: "It's because of my parents."

Still, his buoyant spirits in the aftermath of such a personal tragedy eventually became a cause for concern among some of his doctors. That was most likely because, unlike his parents, relatives, friends, teachers, and coaches, the doctors did not understand his indomitable spirit and religious faith, his refusal to feel sorry for himself or to brook sympathy. "Some of the people at the hospital couldn't understand how a fifteen-year-old kid, with such a bright future in basketball, could possibly stay in such good spirits and not be depressed. But then they didn't know Chris," Linda Samele said. "Then one day they sent in a psychiatrist to talk with him. The psychiatrist was in the room for about an hour. After he had left, Chris asked us, 'Who was that guy?' When we told him, he said, 'He needs help.' And we all laughed."

While young Chris was in the hospital, Jack Watson, the young man whose actions at the accident scene may have saved his life, came often to visit. A close bond developed between the two, despite a ten-year difference in age. The following July, Chris attended Watson's wedding and they became even closer friends. "Chris is a very special kid, a real battler, with tremendous faith and courage," Watson, a State correction officer, said. "He'd get a little discouraged at times. But next thing you knew, his spirits were back up again. He never let the accident get him down."

When he left the hospital on January 18, 1989, Chris Samele weighed ninety-five pounds, forty pounds lighter than when the accident occurred. "One day in early February, he told me he was going over to our old house, which is just around the corner, to shoot some baskets," Linda Samele recalled. "I asked him if he'd like me to come along. But he said, no, he wanted to go alone."

When he got to the house, which his parents still own, Chris put down his crutches, picked up the basketball from inside the garage, and alone with no one in sight began to shoot while hopping around on his right leg. Several times, he lost his balance and fell on the hard asphalt driveway. Each time, he righted himself and kept shooting on his one leg, first from near the basket, then from the foul-line. As more and more shots went in, he thought to himself, *I can still do it. I can still shoot.* After fifteen minutes, he put the ball back in the garage, picked up his crutches, and headed home. "I was curious to see if I still had my shooting touch, and I wondered about my mobility. But when I was done, I felt pretty good. It was my first time out since the accident, and I made more than half of my shots."

From her kitchen, Linda Samele worried about her son's balance. Hoping he would not be disappointed, she could see Chris's shots in the air, but not him, or the basket. "It was a very strange sensation," she said. "I knew Chris felt good about shooting baskets again, but I also knew he had no idea how he would do. When he came home, I asked how it went, and he said, 'I think I shot pretty well, Mom. Everything was okay.'" He never mentioned the falls.

Over the next two months, Chris went to the driveway often, mostly alone, but at times with his mother or father, who would feed him the ball after he had taken a shot. "He had his down days, and when he did, he'd usually say to me, 'Mom, I'm going over to shoot.' At such times, when I asked if he wanted me to go along, he'd say, 'No, I want to be alone.' When he came back, his spirits were always better."

When he wasn't shooting baskets, young Chris was being driven to Waterbury Hospital by his mother for more than one-hundred physical therapy sessions and being tutored at home, as he was at the hospital, to keep up with his school work. He also spent hours lifting weights on a Universal weight set that was given to him by Naugatuck businessman, Dave Morelli. Linda Samele said, "Doug Benedetto, a friend who is in his twenties, brought the weight set over and said to Chris, 'We're going to start working out every day on the weights, and I'm going to be your manager. You're going to come back, I know you are, and I want to help.' I had tears in my eyes. And Doug did it. He'd be in the cellar, yelling, 'Come on, Chris, keep it up. You can do it, I know you can.'"

Chris Samele's comeback effort was not without physical suffering. "At times he was in excruciating pain," his mother said. "He'd rock back and forth while sitting in a chair, but he never complained. He told us it hurt only when we asked him. We also had to increase the strength of his medication to the point of where the next step would have been morphine. Finally, it got so bad that part of a bone on his stump was exposed and he had to go back into the hospital to have an inch and a quarter of the bone removed."

On March 24, 1989, Good Friday, Chris got his first of four prosthetic devices (all without charge) from the Shriners Hospital for Crippled Children in Springfield, Massachusetts. "The first question he asked was whether he could now play basketball," said Ed Skewes, director of the hospital's prosthetic and orthotic department. "I said to him, 'Why don't we get you walking first?' I must say I was dubious about his playing basketball again even with the high-tech prosthetic devices we provided, which were lightweight and had suction sockets and a hydraulic knee unit. But he's a remarkable young man, with tremendous determination and strong family support."

At home in the basement, Chris spent hours practicing walking with his new artificial leg, both forward and backward. As he did, he watched himself in a full-length mirror he had asked his parents to buy. Then a week after he got the prosthesis, he went to the old house to shoot, accompanied by Benedetto. "It was much harder shooting and just moving around with the prosthesis," Chris remembered. "I felt awfully awkward, but I kept at it, even though it didn't feel comfortable until July. And I fell a lot. But most of my shots went in."

By then, Bob Samele knew that his son was on the way back. "He would say to me, 'Dad, I worked too hard and have come too far to quit, even with the accident.' I was amazed at how well Chris was doing in so short of a period of time."

Getting adjusted to a prosthetic device takes time and patience, and it can cause extreme discomfort in the early stages. Indeed, as eager as he was to get his prosthesis, Chris Samele found his new leg so uncomfortable that at times he left it at home, going to school on crutches after having returned to Torrington High in early April of 1989. "When Coach Martin saw me without the prosthesis, I could tell he was annoyed that I wasn't wearing it," Chris said. "After that, I made sure to wear it, no matter how uncomfortable."

By May, though awkward and uncomfortable with his new leg, Chris was playing in some pickup games with friends. Then in late June, Doug Benedetto, his strength "coach," took a team of Torrington High players, including Chris, to play in a tournament at the Word of Life Camp in Schroon Lake, New York, in the Adirondack Mountains. But in the fourth game, Chris, trying to do too much too soon, broke his prosthesis while going after a rebound. He missed the fifth, and last, game, but returned home satisfied. "I did all right, even though I really wasn't ready for competition," he said.

Back home after getting a new prosthesis at the Shriners Hospital in Springfield, Chris embarked on a regimen that included shooting and dribbling alone in the driveway, playing in some pickup games, lifting weights in the basement, and running—forward, backward, and side-to-side—in the backyard. While running, particularly backwards, he fell often, both in the driveway of the old house and in the backyard. But undeterred, he would get up and keep going. *Someday,* he thought, *I'll fall occasionally while playing, just like most guys do, but not like I'm doing now.* And although he was still moving about in a hop-skip motion, dragging his artificial leg, his mobility was definitely improving. As the summer wore on, and his shooting and mobility kept getting better, Chris Samele could hardly wait for the 1989–90 basketball season to begin.

It was December 15, 1989, eight days shy of a year since the terrifying accident that claimed the life of Shawn Collins and cost Chris Samele his left leg. Now it was opening night for the Torrington High basketball season. Though the varsity game between New Milford and Torrington was not to start for another hour and a half, about 250 people already were in the stands at New Milford High School, awaiting the start of the junior varsity game. Normally, about fifty spectators would be on hand for the J.V. game. But this game was special. It marked the beginning of Chris Samele's basketball comeback. To put Chris's return to basketball in perspective, it usually takes about a year before most people can walk comfortably with a prosthesis, let alone play basketball.

When the Torrington junior varsity ran onto the court for pre-game practice, all two hundred or so fans on the Torrington side of the gym stood, cheering and applauding. So too, did most of the New Milford supporters who knew what had happened to Chris Samele. There was no doubt that the ovation was directed at number 23, Chris Samele, easily identifiable by his hop-skip motion, although from the stands it was difficult to discern that his left leg was artificial. "When Chris ran out on the court with us, we all got chills," said teammate and friend Michael Sorvillo. "He was nervous, we knew that; but he was also confident. He knew he could still play."

Among the large Torrington contingent (normally, about seventy-five fans would travel the thirty miles to New Milford for what was a non-conference game, and most would not arrive until the varsity contest was about to start) were Linda and Bob Samele. Emotionally affected, both by the crowd's response and the sight of their son in a Torrington High basketball uniform again, the Sameles fought back tears.

God, please don't let him fall and get hurt, Linda Samele said to herself. *And don't let him be disappointed or embarrassed.*

Well aware of all of the Torrington people in the stands, Chris Samele was visibly nervous. He missed most of his shots during the warm-up session. Then, starting at guard, he was tight and awkward and did not come close to scoring while playing eight of the first thirteen minutes of the sixteen-minute first half. Several of his shots did not even touch the rim of the basket. Usually when that happens, some fans will derisively chant, "Air Ball." But these air balls were met with an uncomfortable silence. Back in the game with two minutes left in the half, Chris took a pass to the left of the basket and, from about twenty feet out, arched a one-handed three-point shot that swished through the hoop. As it did, almost everyone in the gym rose in unison, cheering. "We all breathed a sigh of relief when he made that shot because we knew he was struggling," teammate Sorvillo said. "Chris is a fighter, and we knew he would do okay."

About a minute later, Chris grabbed the rebound of a teammate's shot amid a tangle of arms and flipped the ball into the basket. Again, the crowd exploded. "I felt great after making those two shots, and the crowd made me feel even better," he said a year and a half later. At the half Chris had five points. Much more relaxed, he added six more in the second half—when he fell to the floor once, his only fall of the game—to finish with eleven as the Torrington junior varsity won its opening game. The varsity game, which followed, turned out to be anticlimactic.

"Riding home, Bob and I felt incredibly relieved," Linda Samele said. "We were very nervous and apprehensive for days leading up to and during the first half of the game. But once he made those baskets... I think everyone felt relieved. And to think that all of those people drove to New Milford to see Chris play! That meant a lot to him. And we knew driving back that he had to feel good about his first game."

Chris Samele fell in almost every game, often more than once. But he always got up quickly, checked to make sure his prosthesis was all right, and continued. Jack Watson, the young man who may have saved his life, would look on in amazement. Overall, Chris, who had been named captain by coach Bob Anzellotti, averaged a very respectable twelve points a game, with a high of thirty against the Naugatuck junior varsity when he connected on six three-point shots in a spectacular performance. Rebounding was difficult; defense even more so. In a one-on-one situation, he had to allow between five and six feet between him and his man. "I knew that I had to work hard that summer on moving backward quicker if I was going to play with the varsity," he said.

In the summer of 1990, by then on his fourth artificial leg (he received his fifth, a six-pound, state-of-the-art prosthesis, this past June), Chris worked out daily by himself in the nearby East School, shooting baskets and practicing running leg-over-leg. "My dad told me that, to play with the varsity, I had to run leg-over-leg and not hop and skip, as I did with the J.V." To improve his game and mobility, he played an astounding seventy-five games in three different summer leagues. His play improved dramatically. "He was always getting blisters on his stump," his mother said, "even with four socks over it." With the junior varsity, he shot from the outside in a stationary position. But in the summer leagues he began to use his jump-shot, where both feet left the floor. At first he would jump about two inches off the floor; but by summer's end, he was going as much as six inches in the air off both his real and artificial leg. "After one game in the Pearl Street League in Waterbury (one of the strongest summer circuits in the country), he said to me, 'Dad, did you see what they did to me tonight? They used a box-and-one,'" Bob Samele said with a smile, "and he still scored thirty points, with eight three-pointers." (In a box-and-one defense, four players line up in a zone, while the fifth is assigned to shadow the other team's best player, usually an outstanding shooter).

At the end of the season, Chris was named to the all-star team in the high school division of the Pearl Street League. "That was very good competition, and being named to the all-star team made him feel very good," his father said. There was also another major accomplishment. During the junior varsity season, it would take Chris about thirteen seconds to run the length of the basketball court, a very slow time. By the time school started in September, after endless hours of running up and down the court at the East School both forward and backward, he had cut the time to between six and seven seconds.

Following the junior varsity basketball season the previous

spring, Chris also went out for the varsity tennis team. Though he had only played the game occasionally, and not at all since the accident, he ran up a 12–2 record in doubles on a strong team that had won the Naugatuck Valley championship the previous season. Along with his handicap, Samele was also at a disadvantage because most of the Torrington High tennis players play the game year round, and most had been playing since they were very young. Chris, by comparison, first picked up a tennis racket when he was fourteen years old.

"Considering that he had had his prosthesis for only a year and had such little experience in tennis, Chris absolutely amazed me," the Torrington boys' coach, Eileen Fahey, said. "He moved much better than I thought he would. And he had the best hand-eye coordination I ever saw, and his anticipating was unbelievable. After two weeks of practice, it became obvious that he belonged as a doubles player on what was a very good team."

But basketball remained Samele's first sports love, and during his last two years at Torrington High, with his mobility vastly improved, he led the varsity in three-point baskets, recording twenty during his junior year. Though he continued to fall down from time to time, Chris became increasingly aggressive, driving to the basket often. In one of his final games he scored a game-high seventeen points during a dramatic come-from-behind overtime victory over Sacred Heart High of Waterbury. Indeed, his accomplishments on the court drew the attention of a number of colleges, three of which tried to recruit him for basketball, including Western New England in Springfield, Massachusetts, where he eventually enrolled because the school also expressed an interest in Chris as a tennis player.

As a tennis player, Samele continued to flourish and improve during his final two years at Torrington High. As a junior, he posted a 13–1 record in doubles. Then as a senior, he was determined to play singles and to do so, he had to beat out two teammates. He did, defeating them both in head-to-head competition and then going 7–5 in singles and 9–2 in doubles during his senior year. For his outstanding season, Samele was named the Naugatuck Valley League's Most Valuable Player.

Did he ever have any doubts about being able to come

back and play tennis after losing a leg and never having played on a competitive level? "No, I knew I could do it," he said in his quietly confident manner. "A lot of people didn't think I could ever play basketball again. But I knew that I could, although I also knew I would have to make some adjustments. Same thing with tennis. I realized I'd have to make some changes and anticipate much better. But I knew that I could do it."

Chris Samele's remarkable courage, indomitable spirit, and positive attitude in the aftermath of his devastating injury raised the question as to how he had been able to marshal such inner strength. Asked to explain, he said: "Worse things could have happened to me. I'm lucky to be alive." But where did the inner resolve, the positive attitude, and the confidence come from? "I'm not sure," he answered, "but even since I was small I've always been positive about things. I've never let myself get down. I believe in God and have a lot of faith in him, but that's not the only reason. It's my upbringing, too; the way my parents brought me up."

But why had he worked so hard and endured so much pain to play basketball again, and also tennis, particularly when he knew he could never attain the heights that had been projected for him? "I guess I've tried to prove that you can still be successful in sports, or in anything else, with a handicap if you work hard enough at it," he replied. "And I guess that, to myself, I just wanted to prove that I could still play well. And, also, because of what I've done, I felt that maybe I can be a role model for kids with handicaps. Another reason, I guess, is that, ever since I was a little kid, I worked so hard at becoming a good basketball player. And I felt that even though I'd lost a leg, I had worked too hard to quit."

Sitting in the kitchen of her home, where she was when she received the phone call from Waterbury Hospital on December 23, 1988, Linda Samele recalled driving home from a therapy session at the hospital with Chris and her sisters about two months after the accident that took her son's leg. Suddenly, she recollected, "Chris said, 'Mom, I think I know why this happened to me.' And I said, 'Why, Chris?' And he said, 'It's because God knew that I could handle it.' At that point my sister Marion said, 'Chris, you aren't blaming God for the accident, are you?' And Chris said, 'No, Auntie, God saved my life. But he also knew that I could handle it. And I have and I always will.'"

CHAPTER 2

JENI ARMBRUSTER

Ken Armbruster can't quite recall when his youngest daughter, Jennifer, first picked up a basketball. "It might have been when she was four and I was stationed in Italy, or it could have been the next year when we were at Scott Air Force Base in Illinois," said Armbruster, a retired U.S. Army sergeant. "But I know that once she started playing, she never stopped. And she was good, very, very good." So good in fact that, while Armbruster was stationed in Munich, Germany, between 1982 and 1986, Jeni Armbruster, more often than not, was the only girl on boys' basketball teams and usually was the best player. "In 1985, not only was she the only girl on a championship team, but at the age of ten, she also was the youngest player."

For Jeni Armbruster, no matter the sport—basketball, soccer, softball, field hockey, track and field, volleyball—it all came so easy. And, invariably, she was the best player at any age level as a child, even though in many instances, she was also the youngest. "She was absolutely crazy about sports," Ken Armbruster said. "But she always had a lot of fun playing them, even though she was very competitive." That was the case in Italy, in Germany, and finally in Colorado Springs where the Armbrusters—Ken and Linda and daughters Michelle, Stacy, and Jennifer Dawn—moved in August of 1986 when Armbruster was transferred to Peterson Air Force Base. That September, Jeni entered sixth grade at Horizon Middle School. Although the school did not offer competitive sports until the eighth grade, her talents as an all-round athlete, and particularly in basketball, soon became evident. In virtually every sport she was outstanding, superior to practically all of the other girls and to many of the boys.

"I could see she was something special from the start, even though she couldn't play organized basketball and volleyball until she was in the eighth grade," said Diane Worner, who coached both sports at Horizon.

Playing in the Colorado Springs youth basketball league as a sixth- and seventh-grader, Jeni dazzled teammates, opponents, and coaches with her ball-handling and shooting. She also won numerous medals for her achievements in track and field, mainly in the high jump and the long jump, at that age level and was a star softball and volleyball player. "I could hardly wait to get Jen because I could see she had tremendous potential," Worner said. During the summer of 1988, before becoming eligible for the Horizon School volleyball and basketball teams, Jennifer swept every honor at the Pikes Peak basketball camp in Colorado Springs, where she was named the Outstanding Shooter and King of the Hill (best player in the thirteen-year-old group). Coaches at the camp were unanimous in rating Jeni as the top girls' basketball prospect in Colorado Springs and a sure-fire college star, no doubt good enough to earn a full scholarship to a Division I school. She was only thirteen years old!

Living up to all expectations, Jeni was a sensation in her first year of eligibility at Horizon as an eighth-grader—far and away the best player on the volleyball and basketball teams, especially in basketball, where she averaged more than twenty points a game and was the leading rebounder. "I'd had Jeni in gym classes at Horizon, and in basketball, volleyball, and softball she was far and above the rest of the kids, even most of the boys," Diane Worner recalled. "Needless to say, I was eager to have her on my volleyball, basketball, and track teams in ninth grade. As a coach you dream about having such a player and maybe, if you're lucky, get one once in a lifetime."

Little did Diane Worner, or anyone else for that matter, know that after her eighth-grade year at Horizon, Jeni Armbruster would never be the same player again because of a bizarre affliction that set in the following summer, an affliction which was to change her life but not daunt her spirit.

That summer, in 1989, was one of the busiest of Jeni's young life. Now fourteen years old, she was still recuperating from a dislocated right kneecap, which she had incurred in the high-jump during a track meet the previous spring.

Despite the injury, and the fact that she was not one-hundred percent physically, Jeni attended two basketball camps and played softball, mostly with a team that included her father, mother, and her sister Michelle. Of all her sports, softball was by far the least taxing. It was the sport she played more for fun than anything else, especially on the "family team," and the one least likely to result in a problem. Yet it was during a softball game in July that life, in a sense, changed dramatically for Jeni Armbruster.

"I remember how my dad was pitching and I was in the outfield when, all of a sudden, my right eye got blurry and it started to sting. Before I knew it, I couldn't even see my dad," Jeni recounts. "It stayed like that, and I told my parents about it. But we all thought that I had gotten something in the eye, even though they couldn't see anything, or that a contact had gotten dirty. So when we got home, I took out the contact. But my eye was still blurry and it still stung."

When the condition persisted, the Armbrusters took Jeni to an ophthalmologist who diagnosed the problem as an inflamed optic nerve; but in a matter of weeks, Jeni had lost all sight in her right eye. "It was painful at times and it caused headaches, but we all thought my sight in the eye would come back." Even the eye specialist thought the condition was a temporary one and that the sight in her right eye would be restored. So, too, did a number of other specialists, who also thought the sight-loss was a temporary aberration, but it was not.

By the time Jeni began her ninth-grade classes at Horizon late that summer of 1989, she began to experience a similar blurriness in her left eye. "When I woke up the eye would be blurry, but then as the day went on, it would clear up," she said. "But then one day in September, the fuzziness didn't go away, and I couldn't see at all, except out of the side of my left eye." For all intents and purposes, Jeni Armbruster, in less than two months, had gone blind. Until then, apart from her family, she had told no one, not even her closest friends. "I didn't see any reason to, because I thought it was a temporary thing, and that one day soon the sight in my right eye would come back and everything would be okay." No one noticed. Not even Diane Worner, who after waiting for years, finally was going to be able to coach Jeni on the ninth-grade volleyball and basketball teams.

"Before the volleyball season started, though, Jeni's mom came to me and told me about the problem with her right eye," Worner said. "But even though she was only playing with one eye, Jeni was one of our best players, and we had a pretty good team. Then in September, her mom came to see me again, and this time told me that Jeni had also lost practically all of the sight in her left eye. Obviously now it was hard for her to follow the ball, since she only had some peripheral vision in her left eye. Up until then, she was a starter and played almost the entire game because, even with one eye, she was outstanding. But after Jeni lost sight in the left eye, too, we could just use her as a server, and even there it had to be difficult because she couldn't see the ball. Despite that, she did very well, getting in about forty percent of her serves. And she worked very hard. While the other girls were practicing their spiking, Jeni would be working on her serve against a wall in the gym."

Never did that practice and perseverance pay off more than in a game against Janitell Middle School, a rival from Colorado Springs. Late in the match, in the climactic game, Janitell was within a point of winning at 14–13, and it was Jeni Armbruster's turn to serve. Since a team has to win by at least two points in volleyball, that meant that she had to win three straight points on service, a seemingly impossible task in light of the fact that Jeni could not even see the volleyball when she tossed it in the air to serve. "Jeni, just do the best you can," Diane Worner told her as she got off the bench and was escorted out to the service line by two teammates, which by then had become necessary. "I really wasn't all that worried, because I knew that Jeni was at her best under pressure, which I guess is kind of a strange thing to say when she couldn't even see. But I knew she felt that, 'Hey, the team really needs me to come through now, and I'm going to do it.' That's the type of athlete Jeni is. But, realistically, I felt that this was a very tough assignment for her, since she was a forty-percent server, and she had to serve one-hundred percent on three serves for us to win."

If the atmosphere in the Janitell gym was tense, Jeni Armbruster was not. "I knew it was up to me," she recollected. "At this stage, I wasn't doing anything else but serving, so the least I could do, I felt, was to get in three good serves." The first serve was a bullet that shot across the net and hit the floor before a single Janitell player could get a hand on it. An ace. That tied the score at 14–14. Again Jeni Armbruster tossed a ball that she could not see into the air and, with perfect timing, pounded it across the net like a rifle-shot. Another ace, untouched by any of the opposing players, to give Horizon a 15–14 lead and put it at match-point as the small crowd, including Ken and Linda Armbruster, erupted with cheers. Once again the ball was handed to Jeni Armbruster at the service line. Now there was absolute silence in the gym. Slowly, rhythmically, Jeni again tossed the ball in the air with her left hand and slammed it with her right hand, drilling a line-drive service across the net for another ace, untouched by any Janitell player, to give Horizon a 16–14 victory. Three serves and three improbable aces lifted Horizon from the brink of defeat to one of its most glorious victories. Armbruster was instantly engulfed by her ecstatic teammates.

"They were yelling and screaming," Diane Worner remembered. "It was incredible. And the most amazing thing is that the players on the Janitell team, like kids on other teams we played, didn't even know that Jeni couldn't see."

Worner knew that basketball would present an even greater challenge to the courageous and indomitable five-foot, seven-inch, 130-pound Armbruster. Jeni would not just be able to be the "designated server"—a player who would serve and as soon as the point was over, come out of the game, as she did in the latter part of the volleyball season after losing virtually all of her sight. By then the Armbrusters had taken their youngest daughter to a number of eye specialists—both private ophthalmologists, and Army and Air Force doctors at the Fitzsimmons Army Medical Center in Denver and at the Air Force Academy in Colorado Springs. There were no easy explanations as to what had happened or what the long-range outlook was.

"All they could tell us was that Jeni's condition was known as idiopathic optic neuritis, which was a swelling of the optic nerves that resulted in the loss of sight," Ken Armbruster said. The consensus was that the condition had been caused by a virus, but the doctors said it was rare for both eyes to be affected. They ran a wide range of tests, ranging from brain scans to a spinal tap. Meanwhile, Jeni, unsure of whether her sight would return, began to study

Braille in an effort to keep up with her classmates at Horizon and to continue maintaining a 3.0 average. While the friendly and outgoing blonde teenager learned Braille, teachers gave her tests orally.

"Learning Braille was strange at first, especially since I didn't know if I'd need it for long," she said, "but I picked it up quickly and it certainly helped." Despite her sudden blindness, her grades remained high, so did her spirits. And she stayed on the school's honor roll.

By the time the volleyball season ended in late October, Jeni could barely see at all. She could read enlarged print with a magnifying glass, but even that was difficult. She could still make out some objects with what remained of the peripheral vision in her left eye. After attending regular classes at Horizon, she spent about two hours every day with staff members from the Pikes Peak Board of Cooperative Services, an agency in Colorado Springs, who would teach her Braille and help her adjust to life without eyesight.

"At first, it was tough in class," she recalled during the winter of 1994, at her dormitory room at the University of Northern Colorado in Greeley. "I would just sit there and listen to whatever the teachers said, but couldn't do anything else. Then at night, my parents would have to do all of my reading and writing for me and go over the classwork with me. We'd spend almost the whole evening going over my homework." School officials and the Armbrusters realized that had to change, and it did when a decision was made for her to drop elective subjects and to begin working with the staffers from the Pikes Peak Board.

Given the suddenness of her blindness and the toll it was taking on her at such an important juncture of her life, particularly with her beloved sports, it would have been understandable if Jeni Armbruster became overwhelmed with depression, or even lapsed into depressive moods. But that never happened. "Jeni was disappointed, sure," her father said, "but she never showed any signs of depression."

Was she ever depressed? Jeni was asked in February of 1994 during her freshman year at college. "No. I knew I had to keep on going," she said. "I never saw any reason to say, 'Why me?' I still had my family and friends, and I still had my sports. And, besides, I've always felt that maybe someday my sight will come back."

Because of Jeni's passion for basketball, her father decided to build a concrete basketball court in their backyard in 1989. Ironically, the job was completed in August, shortly after she had lost sight in her right eye and was on the verge of losing most of it in the left eye, too. Jeni still took advantage of the new court, spending hours by herself or with her dad, a former basketball player himself, working on her shooting and her dribbling—even during the late fall when she could barely see the ball and, at times, not see the basket at all. Nothing was going to stop her from playing the game during her last year at Horizon. She knew the team was going to be a good one and she was convinced that, while she'd never again be the player she was in the eight grade when she averaged more than twenty points, she could still be an important contributor.

Still, with most of her sight gone, Jeni understandably had doubts. "Before practice started, she came to me and told me about her concerns," Diane Worner, who also coached the ninth-grade basketball team at Horizon, recalled. "But at the same time she was confident that she could still play. I'm sure that I felt more scared for her than she did for herself. I also felt that deep down she was worried as to whether it was really going to work." Early on during the preseason practice sessions, Diane Worner's fears, and most of Jeni Armbruster's concerns, were allayed. "In some of our drills, Jeni did better than most of the other girls, and her moves were still outstanding. And, being able to see some court markings peripherally from her left eye, she always knew where she was. She had the feel of the whole court. It was absolutely amazing. The main problem, of course, was that she couldn't see the ball. I had to make sure the girls did two important things: call out to Jeni when they were going to pass her the ball, or at least the ball as a fuzzy object; and remember to bounce-passed it to her. She couldn't see the ball at all when it was chest-passed to her. Sometimes, especially early on, the girls would forget and make high passes, which would either go right past her or hit her, sometimes right in the face. On the bounce-pass she could hear the ball coming. Eventually, most of the girls remembered to bounce-pass the ball to Jeni while calling out her name, but sometimes, during the heat of a scrimmage or a game, they'd forget and a pass would hit her in the face and even bloody her nose. It wouldn't faze her at all. She'd go to the locker room to stop the bleeding and come right back out, eager to get back in. And she wouldn't blame anyone. She understood that her teammates sometimes just forgot to bounce-pass the ball."

When the Horizon girl's ninth-grade team opened its season in mid-November of 1989 against Cheyenne Mountain, the tension in the Horizon gym was pervasive. No one was more nervous and apprehensive than Ken and Linda Armbruster. In a way, for their daughter Jeni, this game was a new beginning in basketball. In the pregame warm-ups, Jeni, wearing number 55, made as many shots as she missed, which was remarkable since she could barely make out the outline of the backboard and could not see the basket, even while shooting lay-ups.

"Even though Jeni had done well in practice, I decided not to start her," Diane Worner said, "and I asked her to sit next to me on the bench. We fell behind, and at the end of the first quarter I turned to Jeni and asked if she was ready, and she said she wanted to try, so I sent her in. I remember I got goose bumps as she ran out on the floor, and I'm sure a lot of other people in the crowd did, too. You could just sense that the feeling in the gym was electric."

Within minutes, a teammate whipped a pass towards Jeni—a high pass that she never saw and it sailed over her head, adding to the tension in the gym. Then moments later, Jeni took a bounce-pass just inside the three-point line, squared up toward the basket, and launched an arching one-hand shot, which hit the backboard and dropped through the basket. "It was really an ugly shot and I was off-balance," she said, laughing at the memory. "But I knew it had a chance, and making it meant a lot to me." To her teammates and to the Horizon fans, too. "The kids were jumping up and down and screaming," said Diane Worner. "It was like we had won the N.B.A. championship. And for me, it was an unbelievable thrill, knowing what Jeni had been through and how hard she had worked. It's a basket that I'll never forget." It was to be the only one that Jeni Armbruster was to make that afternoon in the game between two ninth-grade teams, but at least at that moment, it was the biggest one she had ever made. Furthermore, it gave her confidence a needed boost, convincing her anew that she still could not only play basketball, but could score—even though she was shooting at a basket she could see only from memory.

For most of the rest of the season, Jeni was a starting forward, sensing movement by the sound of the ball and what images she was able to discern on the court, rarely making a mistake. "Her ball handling skills were as good as anyone on the team, and maybe even better," Worner said. "And she still had those great moves driving to the basket and played tough defense. It may be hard to believe, but hardly any of the opposing players knew she had lost practically all of her sight. Even most of those who had heard about Jeni couldn't tell during a game which player she was. Quite often a player, or a couple of players, would come over to me after a game and ask, 'Which one's the girl who can't see?' When I'd point out Jeni to them, they'd look at her in absolute disbelief. Overall, Jen played the majority of the time and handled the ball incredibly well. She got frustrated a few times during the season, but she'd get over it quick. And she knew her limitations. She'd say to me, 'I know that I can do this and that, but there are some other things I just can't do anymore.'"

As the season progressed Jeni's condition worsened, testing her resolve all the more on the basketball court. At Christmas she developed a fever that further diminished what little peripheral vision she had left. The Armbrusters took her to the Air Force Academy hospital in Colorado Springs for a week of steroid treatments, to hopefully improve her condition, at least to the point of restoring the lost peripheral vision; but the treatments proved to be unavailing. "After that, Jeni began to have more trouble following the flow of the game and sensing where the ball was," the coach said. "She finally got so frustrated that, near the end of the season, she said to me, 'I don't think I can do it anymore because of the effect the medication has had on me.' I said, 'Are you sure?' And she said, 'Yes.' But she kept coming to the games, sitting on the bench and cheering the other players on. And I knew she felt that she could still play."

About that time, Jeni needed a lift more than ever. In mid-January she got it when the phone rang at the Armbruster home, and she picked it up to hear a voice on the other end of the line say, "Jeni, this is Isiah Thomas."

The Detroit Pistons' star had read about Jeni and learned
that he and Michael Jordan were her favorite players. That
prompted his call, and for about twenty minutes Thomas
and his ninth-grade fan from Colorado Springs chatted about
basketball and obstacles that basketball players, and people
in general, encounter in life. Thomas was to call and write
several times in the years to come, checking up on his new
friend. "It was great when he called," she remembered. "He
even gave me his phone number and said he wanted to stay
in touch. He asked if I was playing, and I told him no
because I was having trouble with my defense, and he said
he often had trouble on defense, too, even with his good
eyesight. We both laughed at that." That winter, Jeni got to
meet Thomas when she and her parents drove to San
Antonio to see the Pistons play. In May she and her father
flew to Portland after Thomas had given them tickets to the
fourth game of the N.B.A. final between the Pistons and the
Portland Trail Blazers. The friendship persisted through high
school and into college, with Jeni often traveling to Denver
to see the great Pistons' guard when the team was in town
to play the Denver Nuggets.

In the meantime, there was no encouraging news about
her continually deteriorating eye condition. After Jeni's last
year at Horizon, the Armbrusters took her to the Washington
University of St. Louis Eye Institute. The prognosis was not
good. "They were the first ones to come right out and say
that there wasn't much chance of me getting my sight back,"
she said. "No one else had ever said that." Once again, the
Armbrusters heard that there was no known cure for Jeni's
affliction. "But I still felt, as I always have, that someday my
sight might come back."

Earlier that spring, though her sight continued to worsen,
Jennifer went out for track, a sport in which she had starred
the previous year at Horizon. "Since she had memorized the
basketball court and got to know it like the back of her
hand, I felt that she could probably handle both the high-
jump and the long-jump, which were her specialties, since
she'd only have to learn to run a specific number of steps
before taking off," said Diane Worner, who also coached
the ninth-grade girls' track team. "And, at that time, Jeni
could still see a little bit."

Before the season began, Jeni slipped and fell before taking off on the high-jump, injuring her wrist. "After that, I didn't do the high-jump anymore," she recalled, "but I did compete in the long-jump with a cast on my wrist." How did she do? "Not that great." But once again the important thing—what really counted—was that Jeni Armbruster kept on competing, barely able to see and with a cast on her wrist.

Aware that her days as a basketball and volleyball player might be nearing an end, Jeni decided in May of that year to try goalball, a sport for blind and nearly blind athletes which includes the principles of soccer and softball. "Lynn Fleharty of the Colorado School for the Deaf and Blind called and told me they were organizing a goalball team and wanted to know if I'd be interested in learning the game," she said. "He'd read about me in the local paper and thought I might want to try the game. So I figured why not?" Played on a volleyball-sized court, with three players on a side, the game employed basketball-sized balls that are equipped with bells. Sidelines are marked with strings so the players can feel them, and the object is to roll the ball through a goal at the end of the court. Adapting to the game quickly, Jeni soon became an outstanding player. She became so good so fast that she was the star of the Colorado goalball team which, that July, was the runner-up in the national goalball championships held in Colorado Springs as part of the annual national games staged by the U.S. Association for Blind Athletes. At the same competition Jeni also won silver medals after finishing second in both the high-jump and the long-jump. Even though Jennifer still had a modicum of sight, it did not help her in goalball, since all competitors are blindfolded during games. "It's a neat sport and it's challenging," she said of the game which was introduced in Germany after World War II as a recreational activity for servicemen who had been blinded in battle. "I liked it right from the start. It's a physical game, and you spend a lot of time on the floor, diving for the ball, like a goalie in soccer, which I had been. So I picked up on it pretty fast."

Almost as remarkable as Jennifer Armbruster's swift development as a goalball player was her father's emergence as a coach in the sport. "I have a background in sports, but I knew nothing about goalball. But Lynn Fleharty told me they needed a coach for the team and asked if I would do it," Armbruster said. "I agreed and then had to take a crash-course in the game, reading up on it and then watching some games."

For a man accustomed to the roar of the crowd at a basketball game, goalball took quite a bit of adjustment, to say the least. "It was really hard for my dad at the start because in goalball everyone watching has to be quiet so the players can hear the ball," Jeni Armbruster said. "I think he almost got an ulcer because he couldn't say anything on the sideline during a game." Armbruster obviously did well as a coach since the Colorado team, after finishing second during his and his youngest daughter's first season. His team also won the silver medal in the national championships the next three years in a row, in addition to winning a number of regional tournaments.

Even though she had developed into a good goalball player during her first year of competition, basketball was foremost on Jeni's mind when she entered Falcon High School as a sophomore in September of 1990. To a lesser extent, so too was volleyball. If anything, her eyesight had deteriorated even further though at that time she could see, albeit very slightly, peripherally out of her left eye. Otherwise there were just blurry lines and shadows and, at times, barely discernible shapes of family members, friends, classmates, teachers, and others. She knew that the high school competition, both in basketball and volleyball, would be much tougher; even making a team would be difficult. This soon became apparent when Jeni was cut from the volleyball team because, as the coach explained to her, her only role could be that of a server and the team could not afford that luxury on the roster. Disappointed, but not totally surprised at being cut, Jeni began to practice harder than ever for basketball, a game in which she was convinced she could still be a complete player.

"I knew I could still shoot, and I knew I could pass the ball and catch passes, as long as the other girls called out to me," she said. "I also knew I could still play defense, especially when we used a zone, which we usually did, and I certainly could dribble. After all, you're not supposed to look at the ball when you dribble, anyway."

The Falcon High girls' junior varsity coach, Rich Bellew, knew all too well that Jeni Armbruster could do all of these things, and do them very well. "We were looking forward to Jeni playing with us," Bellew said. "I thought that on the middle-school level, even though she could hardly see, she was the best player in the area. And I thought that even with her limitations, she was the finest player we had in the whole program. Jeni certainly had the best skills."

Though she played well during her two years with the Falcon junior varsity, she played sparingly, averaging about a quarter a game. "Jeni's main problem was in the open court," said Bellew who went on to become the girls' varsity coach at Falcon High. "And she had a hard time discerning players, as to whether they were teammates or opponents. But Jeni still handled the ball very well and still shot well, hitting on about twenty percent of her shots, which is not bad at all, since at the junior varsity level anything over thirty-five percent is very good. Overall, Jeni certainly never hurt us and in some aspects of the game, she was great, such as in dribbling through her legs or behind her back. And she still had great moves. In one game she scored eleven points, and on one of her baskets she put a great move on a defender, went around her and put in a reverse layup. But sometimes she would get down on herself. I guess she'd be thinking of what might have been. At such times, I could see the hurt in her eyes and in those of her parents, who are such wonderful people. But overall she had such a great attitude. I remember once when a former Falcon player, Ralph Muldanaro, was home from college and shooting in the gym with Jeni. Knowing what she was going through, Muldanaro took some shots with his eyes closed and then said, 'Hey, Jen, this is really hard.' And she answered, 'It's no big deal; I do it all the time.'"

Still, Jeni Armbruster came away from her two seasons with the junior varsity disappointed and afraid that, unless her sight was to return, she probably would never play competitive basketball again. "It was very frustrating. And the biggest problem was convincing the coaches that I could still play. Yet I don't blame them for limiting my playing time. I can understand how they felt." Meanwhile, she continued looking for new challenges. Though only a novice bowler, Jeni won a bowling tournament during her sophomore year and began to attack intermediate ski slopes in the Colorado Springs area with both skill and passion.

(Usually, blind skiers follow the sounds of a "guide" skier, but Jeni has preferred to have her guide skier stay directly in back of her instead, calling out commands when necessary). In February of her sophomore year, she was selected to attend an elite goalball camp, and that summer played with the U.S. National Team at the National Championships for the Disabled, where she also won the javelin. After attending the camp, she excelled with the national team, finishing as the second leading scorer during a five-game series against Canada. The following February, during her junior year at Falcon High, she was named the Most Valuable Player at the U.S. Association for Blind Athletes National Goalball Tournament in Indianapolis. Similar MVP honors also were bestowed on her at goalball tournaments in Kalamazoo, Michigan, and in Lansdale, Pennsylvania. In March she was named Colorado's "Sportswoman of the Year" for 1991 by the Sportswomen of Colorado who, citing her remarkable achievements both as an athlete and a student, described her as "an athlete who knows that attitude is everything in life—the indomitable Jennifer Armbruster."

But the year of 1992, as it developed, was to be a year of mixed blessings, of triumphs and setbacks, of wondrous achievement, and demoralizing adversity. Of all the honors accorded Jeni that winter, the most noteworthy was her selection as a member of the U.S. Goalball Team for the 1992 Paralympics for Disabled Athletes in Barcelona, which took place two weeks after the Olympic Games and at the same venues. Before leaving for Barcelona, Jeni received yet another honor when she was named the Most Valuable Player at the Southwest Goalball Regional championships in Colorado Springs.

Then two days before she was to depart for Barcelona, the same symptoms that had occurred three years earlier—a stinging sensation coupled with flashes of pain—returned in her left eye. Within twenty-four hours, the vision that had remained in the eye was gone and Jeni Armbruster, at the age of seventeen, was totally blind. This shocking development did not deter the indomitable teenager. "I was going to have to play with a blindfold anyway, because those are the rules for everyone," she recalled. "And I was so pumped up about going to Barcelona that I don't really think it (the loss of her little remaining sight) affected me." Jennifer Armbruster left for Barcelona, where she was to be the youngest blind athlete and the second youngest athlete overall on the 503-member U.S. team at the Paralympics.

Despite the enormity of her latest setback, Jeni performed brilliantly in Barcelona, leading the U.S. team to a fifth-place finish, tying for scoring honors on her team, and finishing fourth in the tournament. "The level of competition was incredible," she said in referring to the twelve-nation event at the Paralympics, which drew 4,000 disabled athletes from eighty-five nations. "Now we can look forward to the '96 Olympics in Atlanta."

Coaches and players were amazed at how well Jeni Armbruster did at the Paralympics considering that she had only been playing the game for two years. She got much better, winning MVP honors at four tournaments in 1993, including the U.S. National Championships in June, the month she graduated from Falcon High as a member of the National Honor Society. Earlier that year, Jeni took time off from Falcon High to attend the Seeing Eye School in Morristown, New Jersey, where she met her new guide dog. In the years to come, Eloise became not only an extremely close companion and friend, but also her roommate at the University of Northern Colorado. As if all of that weren't enough for a teenager trying to adjust to the loss of her sight, Jeni became heavily involved with SportsMates, a program founded by Denver Broncos' football star Karl Mecklenburg to assist physically-handicapped young athletes. With Mecklenburg, she helped raise more than $100,000 for the U.S. Association for Blind Athletes. She did even more by becoming a leader in two drug education programs for teenagers in the Colorado Springs area.

By the time, Jeni Armbruster got to the University of Northern Colorado as a freshman in August of 1993, her basketball and volleyball days were over, barring a near-miracle in the years to come; but she was well on her way to conquering another sport—goalball. "Jeni is already the best female goalball player in the country, and she's only nineteen years old," Tom Parrigin, the coach of the U.S. Blind Athletes Association National Goalball Team, said in February of 1994. "And she's probably in the top ten or top fifteen in the world, which is quite remarkable since most goalball players don't reach their primes until their mid or late twenties."

At Northern Colorado, she trained assiduously, working out with the track team, lifting weights, and exercising on a Stairmaster and stationary bicycle. Colorado being Colorado, winter produced tons of snow, and drew Jeni Armbruster to nearby ski slopes often. While her main sports focus was on goalball, occasionally she would pick up a basketball in the gym and, with a friend, shoot some hoops. No longer were there any floor markings that she could see peripherally from her left eye, but from memory, she could almost instinctively sense where she was on the court and send shots swishing through the basket.

"I don't think Jeni realizes the impact she's had on some people, both other kids and grownups, too," Richens Smith, the principal at Horizon Middle School, said. "She raised kids to another level of awareness and inspired everybody. And she certainly never looked for sympathy. She is truly remarkable."

For many young people, what happened to Jennifer Dawn Armbruster would have been an incomprehensible, and a devastating nightmare that would have led to years of overwhelming sorrow and self-pity. But to Jeni Armbruster the experience became another challenge to accept and to overcome the best she could with the help of caring classmates, coaches, and a deeply-loving and close-knit family. Also there was her and her family's deep abiding faith.

"If God meant for this to happen to me, I guess he did because he knew I could handle it, and I know I can," she said with her guide dog, Eloise, at her side in late winter of 1994. "And I've accepted it, although I'd give anything to have my sight back. And maybe some day that will happen. But in the meantime it's strange but I've seen things I'd never seen before, and heard stories and met people I wouldn't have if this hadn't happened. It's all opened my eyes in a different sort of way. And I've learned to listen more closely, to pay closer attention. You find yourself doing that when you've lost your sight. And look where I've been— to the Paralympics in Barcelona and to so many other places that I otherwise probably never would have gone to. And I probably never would have met Isiah Thomas, who became my friend. I've also got a wonderful family and a lot of great friends. So I've got a lot to live for. And if my sight comes back, that would be great. I know that I'll never give up hope."

Nor will anyone else who has come in touch with this courageous young woman whose positive attitude has never wavered and whose competitive spirit cannot be diminished despite the adversity she had endured. After all, this is Jeni Armbruster who cleared high-jump bars she could not see, served aces across volleyball nets that she knew only from memory, and shot successfully at baskets that she also could not see after catching passes she could only hear.

CHAPTER 3

DENNIS WYCHOCKI

Growing up on the far southeast side of Chicago, Dennis Wychocki wasn't much different than most other kids his age in the blue-collar, working man's neighborhood known as Hegewisch. Crazy about sports, he played them all—baseball, football, basketball, soccer, and hockey. Fun-loving and adventurous, he also rode a bike, swam, and fished in Wolf Lake near his home, and roughhoused with his two older brothers and his many friends. No, Dennis Wychocki was no different than the other kids, except for one thing: he had no arms.

In truth, young Dennis hardly noticed. Nor did his friends who accepted him as just one of the kids, able to do just about everything except carry his books which they were more than glad to do for him. If Dennis had a handicap, no one seemed to notice. That was just fine with Leonard and Rosemary Wychocki who, from the time Dennis was born, treated him like a normal kid, difficult as that sometimes was. "When Dennis was born, it was difficult for my wife and me to understand at first, since our two other sons were perfectly normal, and nothing like this had ever happened in our families," Leonard Wychocki said. "But we decided right away that we were not going to treat Dennis as a handicapped kid, but as a normal kid, who would play and go to school with normal kids. There were to be no special handicapped schools for Dennis."

Still, it would take time. "We realized at first that Dennis was different," Rosemary Wychocki recalled. "After all, he had no arms. But the more we looked at him, the more we realized that he was a cute baby who looked like any other baby. And until he was five years old, I didn't do anything different for Dennis than I had for our other sons. After that, the biggest difference was that we had to help Dennis get dressed and tie his shoes. Otherwise, he could do everything our older sons could."

Some things were tougher than others, such as riding a bike with no hands. While riding his brother Gary's bike when he was about eight, Dennis took a bad spill, hitting his head on a sidewalk. "He was knocked unconscious," his father said, "and I realized I had to do something to make it easier for Dennis to ride a bike. So I rigged up the handlebars so that he could operate them with his chest muscles. In a way the steering was similar to the way anti-aircraft guns are fired, by using the chest and shoulder muscles. It's something I remembered from my days in the Coast Guard during World War II. After that, I also gave him a motorcycle helmet and told him he had to wear it. He didn't like to wear the helmet, but at least he didn't fall off the bike anymore so far as I know."

Doing most other things with his friends was somewhat difficult, not that Dennis ever complained. "Dennis never complained about anything, and certainly not about not having any hands," said a close boyhood friend, Alan Bednarek, a Chicago policeman who still lives in the old neighborhood. "He never thought of himself as handicapped. And as far as I was concerned, he didn't have a handicap. He could do everything the rest of us could." In baseball, Dennis was pitcher, and a pretty good one at that. A pitcher with no hands? Yes, with no hands. "Dennis would roll the ball up on his left foot and flip it in," Bednarek recalled, "and he could do it real fast. It wasn't that easy getting a hit off of him."

Basketball was somewhat harder, so much so that Dennis could not play the game on a regular competitive basis. But, fooling around with his friends, he could match them basket for basket in shots beyond the "key" by shooting the ball into the hoop with his left foot from as far away as half-court. "For me, the farther away from the basket, the better," he said in an interview in the spring of 1994. Horseshoes were a bit easier, even though Dennis had to flip them with his foot, but he became very proficient at the game.

Football was perhaps Dennis' most difficult sport of all. After all, how in the world can you play football if you can neither throw nor catch the ball nor make a tackle? Yet, as it turned out, it became his best sport. "My friends made up a special rule when I started to play touch football with them in the street," he said. "I was a wide receiver, and if a pass hit me in the chest, it was considered a completion." This meant that when a pass had bounced off Dennis Wychocki's chest he would keep running, sometimes for a touchdown without the ball.

Dennis knew that if he wanted to play football at a higher level, say in high school, opposing coaches would not be as magnanimous in bending the rules in his favor. So as he got into his early teens he began to focus on kicking the football, particularly placekicking—the art of kicking extra points and field goals. Punting was out of the question, since in order to punt, you've got to be able to catch the snap from the center, and in Dennis' situation that was impossible. So, with friends acting as his "holder" or using makeshift tees that he could kick off of, Dennis spent hours practicing his placekicking. Before long, Dennis, who was always tall for his age, was not only kicking a football very far, but very high. "Since we usually played in the street, we didn't have goal posts for me to aim at, so I would aim at street lights, trying to kick the ball over the lights," he recalled. "After a while, it became easy." As is the case with many football placekickers, a soccer background helped. "I was a pretty good soccer player, and had developed a strong left leg," he said. "But unlike most soccer players who become placekickers, I always used the old straight-ahead style of kicking, rather than the sidewinder style [wherein kickers approach the ball from an angle, much as they kick a soccer ball]."

If kicking a football was easy for Dennis, such mundane things as eating, drinking, writing, and drawing were not. "We got Dennis an artificial left arm when he was about two, and he wore it off and on through high school," his father said. "But he found it too cumbersome—for one thing it was solid plastic and weighed about ten pounds and it made his shoulder sweat a lot—and in high school he hardly ever used it." Most of the time, Dennis used his mouth and toes to write and to draw. To eat, he primarily relied on the one finger he had which was attached to his right shoulder. "Sometimes we'd help him, like maybe hold a sandwich for him while he ate," Alan Bednarek said. "And I'd usually carry his books while we walked to school."

Alan Bednarek and other friends were usually around to help Dennis in other ways, too. Dennis loved to fish in Wolf Lake, but had trouble casting. "I'd usually cast out the line for him, and then he would reel it in with his feet," Bednarek said. "And he could reel in the line very fast. Sometimes he'd want to cast himself, so he'd put the rod under his chin and kind of thrust the line out. We'd spend a lot of time fishing for bass and blue gill in the lake during summer vacation, and I knew how much Dennis loved to fish."

If Alan Bednarek was helpful to his best friend, so too was Dennis helpful to Alan, to the point of maybe saving his life. "One winter when we were about eleven, Dennis and I went down to the lake," Alan recalled. "And although my parents had told me not to go on the ice because they thought it might be thin, I went out on it at the deep part of the lake. Suddenly, the ice gave way and I went right through and into the water. Dennis ran right over, sat down on the edge of the ice, and flipped his legs towards me, hollering for me to grab his legs. I did, and he yanked me up out of the water. I'll never forget that."

Hegewisch, where Dennis grew up, was a tough, old-fashioned neighborhood populated mainly by Eastern European immigrants and their families, most of them of Polish descent, like the Wychockis. On the southeastern tip of Chicago, bordering Hammond, Indiana, and Calumet City, Illinois, Hegewisch is also bordered by sprawling railroad yards and steel mills. In the distance is the Chicago skyline, seemingly so near and yet, to most people in Hegewisch, so far away. In such neighborhoods in the 1960s and 1970s, when Dennis Wychocki was growing up, kids still made their own fun for the most part, organizing pickup games in baseball, football, basketball, soccer, and ice hockey, more often than not without skates, which were a luxury item in Hegewisch. Sports were the lifeblood of kids like Dennis, enabling them to expend their youthful energy in a competitive fashion, to help forge friendships, and to help stay out of trouble.

But if most of the kids in Hegewisch were tough-hewed, they were also fair. They might trash-talk opponents from time to time, but never denigrate anyone because of physical frailty; that was always the case with Dennis. Friends might occasionally engage in some black humor relating to his handicap, but it was always good-natured and never hurtful. "I don't remember anyone ever taunting Dennis, and I've known him since kindergarten," Alan Bednarek said. "Everybody just accepted him the way he was. It was like he didn't have a handicap at all, and there he was without arms."

Sometimes though, Dennis tried to do too much. "If he couldn't do something, he would try, try, and keep trying until he succeeded," Bednarek said. "And sometimes we would encourage him too much." Like the time Alan, Dennis, and some other friends were playing down near Wolf Lake. "We had tied a rope up on a tree and would swing back and forth on a branch, while grabbing onto the rope. Dennis wanted to try it, which was pretty risky, but he wanted to do it. So he grabbed the rope with his chin, we gave him a shove on the branch, and off he went, about ten feet off the ground. It was scary to watch, but he loved it. We realized right away that we better not let him do that again. But then that was Dennis. He wanted to do everything we did, and we got to a point where we felt he could do anything."

That's just the way Dennis wanted it to be. "I never felt I was different," he said at his Chicago home, about two miles from the old neighborhood, in March of 1994, two months after he had turned thirty-three. "I always felt that I could find a way to do the things my friends were doing. And I don't ever remember anyone taunting me or making fun of me. Sometimes things would be said about my handicap that I couldn't hear. But I'd know somebody was saying something about me because I'd hear Alan or one of my other close friends say, 'What are you talking about? He can do more things than you can.' So I guess friends like Alan or John Allen Kaim were always protecting me, always looking out for me, even when I wasn't aware of it."

Given his consuming interest in sports, it would be understandable if Dennis envied his able-bodied friends, but he said it never happened. "When I was still a very young kid, going to St. Columbia Parochial School, I began to realize that this is the way God wanted me to be, and I accepted it. I never felt envy or resentful, and why should I? I could do everything my friends could do, even though, for me, it might sometimes be harder. But I could still do them, and I had a great boyhood, a lot of fun with a lot of great friends. We were always doing something, and it usually involved sports."

By the time he got to the sixth grade at St. Columba, Dennis realized that if he had any future in sports it would be in football. "I liked soccer, and was pretty good at it," he said, "but it wasn't a big game in our neighborhood. The kicking appealed to me, and I used to spend hours practicing by myself, kicking a soccer ball against our house on Avenue L which was made of brick. But my dad finally made me stop because I was knocking some of the mortar loose on the house. Then as I got more interested in football, I would practice placekicking in the driveway off a tee, aiming at specific trees, both for accuracy and so the ball would bounce back to me."

It was while he was in the sixth grade that Dennis, along with his friends, got to play for an organized sports team for the first time—the Hegewisch Bulldogs, a team made up of kids from the neighborhood that entered the Chicago Park League. "I was the placekicker," he recalled. "But we didn't have a very good team and didn't score too many touchdowns, so I rarely got in to kick extra points." But just wearing a football uniform for the first time, the excitement of it all, and the competitiveness convinced Dennis that this was going to be his sport. Unfortunately, Dennis was only able to play in the Park League that one season. Always big for his age, by the time the next season began, he was over the 120-pound weight limit for the league, and could not play organized football when he was in the seventh and eighth grades. "But I kept practicing, looking ahead to high school, and I got better and better." Word of Dennis' prowess as a placekicker had reached some coaches in the strong Chicago Catholic League well before he got to high school. "I first heard about Dennis when he was in the seventh grade, and then I talked to him the following year," said Dick Marin, the former freshman football coach at St. Francis de Sales High School in Chicago.

Wychocki remembered the conversation. "As I recall, Coach Marin came to St. Columba to try to get kids interested in going to St. Francis de Sales. But I guess he was also looking for football players because they had a strong football tradition. And he did talk to me to see if I was interested, which I was."

Even though Marin had heard a lot about Dennis as a kicker, he admitted later he had some doubts. *How am I going to handle this if he does come out for football?* he thought to himself. But Bob Savage, the father of one of Dennis' classmates at St. Columba, who had recommended Dennis to Marin, told the coach he had nothing to worry about and that young Wychocki could handle himself just fine on the football field.

Marin found that out before the following season began after Dennis decided to go to de Sales, which like Hegewisch, is situated in a blue-collar neighborhood surrounded by factories, railroad yards, a ship canal, and the nearby Chicago skyline. In preseason drills, he did wind sprints and all of the other exercises except for pushups. "The only other thing Dennis couldn't do was dress himself, so we helped put on his shoulder pads and the rest of his uniform," said Bill Miller, who first met him at de Sales and would ultimately be his holder for four years at the school. "If anything, just the sight of him doing all of the calisthenics and just about everything else, made us work harder. You certainly never thought of him as being handicapped."

At home, Dennis' parents were split in their reaction to his going out for football. Leonard Wychocki knew that the Chicago Catholic League was one of the best high school football conferences in the country and that many of the football players were both big and strong, going on to play at colleges with major football programs. "We were concerned with Dennis playing sports, especially football, but yet we knew how much sports meant to him," said his father who, along with his wife, bought a farm in Rensselaer, Indiana, following his retirement after thirty-seven years as a maintenance man at General Mills in Chicago. "And then too, he was only going to be a placekicker, so I felt it might be okay."

So did Dennis' older brothers, Leonard Jr. and Gary, who were solidly behind him as an athlete. Rosemary Wychocki, like most mothers, was apprehensive about football and all the more so because of her son's handicap, which she felt was much too severe for a contact sport. "I was dead-set against it because I was afraid Dennis might get hurt," she said. "But I was outnumbered by all the men in the house. Even our dog was a male."

At six-feet and 140 pounds, Dennis was bigger than most members of an outstanding de Sales freshman team, which won all ten of its games. Establishing himself as the team's best placekicker before the season began, Dennis made good on forty-seven of fifty-five extra-point attempts. "I could tell right away that Dennis was going to become one of the best placekickers de Sales ever had," Marin said. As a freshman, Wychocki was already so good that he also spent some time with the varsity—highly unusual for a freshman player at de Sales—and was the placekicker for the sophomore and junior varsity teams as well. "Sometimes, I'd play four games in one week," he recalled, "and I loved it."

From Marin's perspective, Dennis loved the game a little too much for his own good. "I'd tell him to run off the field when there was a bad snap from center and he couldn't kick," the former coach said. "But he wouldn't do it; he wanted to stay right out there and help if he possibly could. And he was constantly asking me to let him kick off, which I wouldn't let him do, but which he did later. Dennis was a great competitor and I couldn't say enough about his determination and his ability."

In the following summer of 1976, Dennis worked harder than ever on his kicking. With Bill Miller, who had quarterbacked the undefeated freshman team and had been Wychocki's holder, Dennis spent hours at Calumet Park, not far from Hegewisch, practicing extra points and field goals. Miller meanwhile, who would go on to become the varsity quarterback and one of Dennis' best friends, would have him run pass routes and throw passes to him, which Wychocki of course could never catch. "But if Bill's passes hit me in the chest, we regarded them as completions, just like we used to do playing touch in the street," Dennis said.

"I never saw anyone work as hard at football as Dennis did, whether it was during the season or in the summer," said Miller who went on to play football at Dubuque College in Iowa before joining a security firm in Chicago and serving as an assistant football coach at de Sales High School. "And, like I said, it rubbed off on the rest of us and made us work harder."

Mike Mannott, who was to coach Dennis as a senior, vividly recalled Dennis' work ethic. "On hot days in August during preseason drills, he'd work so hard that you'd think he was out for linebacker," Mannott recalled. "He was just incredible, both in his ability and in his all-round attitude."

In general, athletes at de Sales had to work harder since, in the Chicago Catholic League, the school was vastly outnumbered in terms of students.

"We had less than five hundred kids at de Sales," Miller said, "and our school was co-ed. Yet we had to compete against other schools that had as many as two thousand kids, all of them boys." Fortunately for its coaches, de Sales, in large measure because of its strong sports tradition, attracted many outstanding athletes, a lot of them very good football players. "The kids who came knew they'd be playing in one of the best leagues in the country," said Miller. "And the football team had a winning tradition."

During his last three years at de Sales, the football team continued to have a winning record. As a sophomore, Dennis was again extraordinarily busy as the primary placekicker for the sophomore and junior varsity teams and in several varsity games. As a junior and senior he came into his own as the regular placekicker for the varsity. He developed into the best extra point and field goal kicker in the Chicago Catholic League, scoring ninety-eight points on his placekicks and never missing an extra point. He had also bulked up considerably, weighing about 175 pounds by his senior year, thirty-five more than when he arrived at de Sales. Much stronger, he was booming kickoffs into the end zone.

"Dennis always wanted to kick off, but it wasn't until his junior year that I let him do it on a fairly regular basis," said John Cappello, the varsity coach during Dennis' sophomore and junior years. "First I went to his father and asked if he was concerned about having Dennis kick off," Cappello, now a guidance counselor at de Sales, said. Cappello knew, as did Leonard Wychocki, that the kickoff man is occasionally expected to at least try to make a tackle, usually when the kick returner had eluded the other ten opponents and the kicker was the only man between him and the goal line.

Also at times, blocks are thrown at the kickoff man by downfield blockers. Such blocks can be punishing, to say the least. Leonard Wychocki, who never missed one of his son's games during his four years at de Sales, knew of those inherent dangers. He also knew that Dennis wanted desperately to kick off, besides kicking extra points and field goals. "If he wants to, let him do it," he told the coach. Apprehensive as he was about the prospect of Dennis kicking off, those words were just what Cappello wanted to hear. "Okay, I'll let him kick off, Mr. Wychocki," he said. "But I'll also tell him to be careful out there."

The coach did indeed tell Dennis Wychocki just that, but he could tell by the smile on his face that the advice fell on deaf ears, as he knew it would. "Sure, coach, I'll be careful," Dennis said, smiling. "But with this great bunch of players we've got here, I'm not going to have to tackle anybody anyway." Now, Coach Cappello was smiling, too. Cappello thought to himself, *This is the most mature seventeen year-old kid I've ever known.*

Inevitably, it happened. The opponent was Loyola Academy, a longtime rival, who the Pioneers (de Sales' nickname) were playing on Homecoming Day in 1977 during Wychocki's junior year. A big crowd was on hand, and Dennis did not want to disappoint the de Sales fans. He sent the opening kickoff soaring into the Loyola end zone, where one of the deep-back receivers caught it and began sprinting up the middle. Suddenly, he shifted to his left and broke into the clear, racing down the left sideline until one player stood between him and the de Sales' goal line—Dennis Wychocki, the placekicker with no arms. It was the moment Dennis had waited for—an opportunity to show that he was not just a kicker, but a football player. Zeroing in on the receiver as he crossed midfield and moved into the Pioneers' territory, Dennis caught up with him near the forty-yard line and, thrusting forward, head down, sent the Loyola ball carrier flying out of bounds as his helmet crashed into his lower body. The crowd roared, deliriously happy for the least likely of football players, who had just averted a touchdown. As it developed, it was the play of the game since de Sales went on to win by a touchdown. "Do I remember it?" Wychocki asked seventeen years later. "You bet I do. To me it was extremely important that I made the tackle because there was no way I wanted the ball carrier to ruin our homecoming."

Bill Miller also remembered the tackle vividly. "Everyone was going crazy after Dennis made it, but when he came to the sideline, he was very calm. But then that's the way he always was during a game. No matter how crucial the kick, he was completely calm. Nothing ruffled him. And if he felt any pressure, he sure didn't show it."

Though it seldom occurred when he was on the field, Dennis reveled in the physical contact. When he did make contact, such as his touchdown-saving tackle against Loyola Academy, it was usually memorable. Bill Miller remembered another play in particular. "We lined up for a long field goal, which I think everyone on the other team knew was going to be a fake," the one-time de Sales quarterback reminisced. "Then as I took the ball from center while kneeling as the holder for Dennis, I started to take off. As I did, two linemen broke through and Dennis leveled both of them with a crushing block, and I gained about forty-five yards. I don't think Dennis was trying to prove anything; he just saw these guys bearing down on me and felt that he had to do something, and the only thing to do was to throw a block, which he did, and it was a beauty."

Mainly though, Dennis Wychocki was a non-contact placekicker who, as a junior, accounted for all of de Sales' points in one game when he booted four field goals, and as a senior, kicked three field goals, one in overtime, as the Pioneers beat Weber High. "And Dennis' kick made the difference in my last game as a coach in 1977, when as a junior, he kicked the extra point that beat Mt. Carmel, our biggest rival, 7–6," John Cappello remembered. "I couldn't think of a better way of ending my career as a coach."

As a tribute to his kicking excellence, Dennis was named the best kicker in the Chicago Catholic League following his senior season when the Pioneers finished with a 6–3 won-lost record. "That was something special," he said years later, "especially since it's such a strong league and there were so many good placekickers in it. It was quite an honor."

Following his high school career, Dennis never played in another football game. "He could have, though," said Bill Miller, the Pioneer quarterback and Wychocki's holder during their years at de Sales. "I know that Dubuque, a Division III school where I played, tried to recruit Dennis, but he wasn't interested. Could he have played at that level? I certainly think so. After all, he was the best placekicker in the Chicago Catholic League, and that's a very, very good league."

After graduating from St. Francis de Sales in 1979, Dennis enrolled at DePaul University in Chicago, his football playing days behind him. But then fate dealt Dennis another severe blow when, in March of 1980, he was diagnosed with testicular cancer. He underwent the first of two operations that April and was in and out of hospitals for much of the next two years, as his weight dropped from 175 to 145 pounds. Chemotherapy and other treatments proved successful, and by the fall of 1982 he was back in school at Thorton Junior College in Chicago, where he attended for two years. After spending a year at the University of Illinois in Chicago, Dennis took a job as a project manager for an engineering firm. "But then the recession hit and I was let go," he said. "By then I was married and my wife, Sue, and I decided that the best thing for me was to go back to school and get my degree, which I did. If all goes well, I should graduate from the University of Illinois in 1996 with a degree in mechanical engineering."

Nowadays for relaxation, Wychocki fishes (a longtime passion), swims, and bowls, scoring as high as 150 while bowling with his left foot which is higher than many bowlers do with their hands. Another hobby, which stems from his days as a teenager in Hegewisch, is tinkering with cars. "Dennis always liked tinkering with cars, and he knew what he was doing," his father recalled. "If a friend had a problem with a car, Dennis would offer to try to fix it, or if the car needed it, tune it up—with his toes."

The fascination with cars has persisted. "He still loves to work on cars, whether it's tuning them up or rotating the tires, which he does for our two cars," his wife, Susan, said. "There's not anything I know of that Dennis can't do, except the dishes and washing clothes, and in both cases he used his maleness as an excuse."

As a special education teacher, Susan Bachman Wychocki can particularly appreciate all of the things that her husband can do. The first thing was watching him drive a car while steering with his left foot. "We met at a mutual friend's wedding in 1989," she recalled. "The guy I had gone to the wedding with had had too much to drink, and a friend of mine suggested that Dennis drive me home. But then the friend told me, 'He drives a car, but he has no arms.' I said, 'What?' And my friend said, 'Don't worry; he's a good guy and a good driver.' Then he introduced me to Dennis, and I told him I'd love to see his car. He showed it to me and showed me how he steered with his foot. Well, he exuded so much confidence that I wasn't concerned at all, and I let him drive me home. The next week we started dating, and three years later we got married. The funny thing is how I remember, when Dennis was in high school, my father looked up from the paper one day and said, 'Look at this story. This guy has no hands and he plays football.' Well, at the time I wasn't much into sports and so I wasn't impressed. But then when Dennis drove me home after the wedding, I said to my father, 'Dad, you remember that guy you read about who was playing football with no hands? He drove me home and I think I'm going to go out with him.' You should have seen the expression on my father's face."

Looking back, Dennis Wychocki has no regrets, either about his life or the fact that he was born without hands. "I never felt sorry for myself," he said. "There never was any reason to as far as I was concerned. Some parents hide their kids when they have a disability. But mine didn't. They always made me a part of everything they did, and they brought me up as a normal kid, which I always considered myself to be. I never felt that I was 'different.' And I don't think my friends did, either. And I know I could have been a lot worse off. Right through high school, I used to have to go to the University of Chicago Hospital every once in a while for a checkup. When I was there, I'd see kids with multiple problems—kids who were a lot worse off than me. So I couldn't see feeling sorry for myself."

What if he had arms? Would things have been a lot different? He smiles at the questions. "Well for one thing, if I had arms, with my size in high school, I probably would have been a running back and not a kicker. That would have been nice. But then it was nice being a kicker. No regrets about that."

Then Dennis Wychocki recalled his last "kick."

"It was at my wedding," he said, laughing. "Bill Miller, who'd been my holder in high school, was there. I'd been the best man at his wedding, and now he was a member of my wedding party. And when it came time for the groom, me, to put the garter on my bride, Bill knelt down on the floor at the reception, holding the garter as if it were a football, and I kicked it right out into the crowd. Straight down the middle."

CHAPTER 4

DAVID POTTER

At the age of eleven, playing in the Spring Branch National Little League in Houston, Texas, David Potter batted a gaudy .429 and finished the season with a .733 on-base percentage, meaning he reached base about three of every four times he got to bat. Remarkable? Not particularly for a good Little Leaguer, but astounding for David since he has no hands or forearms and hasn't since he was four years old when he touched a live transformer while playing with some friends.

But then, even in spite of the accident which practically burned off both of his arms, David Potter could always hit a baseball, either while playing informal games with friends in neighborhood lots or in organized games. The problem wasn't hitting. David could do that just fine by cradling the bat handle under his left armpit while resting the shaft on the crook of what little remained of his right arm, and then, with all of the power his young body could muster, lashing out at the baseball. The problem also wasn't catching the ball, which David could do just about as well as any other Little Leaguer his age, with a glove that he wore on the stump of his left arm just below the elbow. No, the problem was throwing because how can anyone be expected to throw a baseball, or any other thing, for that matter, without a hand? Not even David Potter, the kid who could hit .429 with no hands, could do that. Shoot a basketball maybe, or even catch a football. But throw a baseball with no hands? No way. So when David caught a baseball, he sort of wound up with the ball in his glove, and shotputted it in towards the closest infielder. Understandably, the ball never went very far. And that was David's greatest frustration as a ballplayer, otherwise he could do it all: hit, run the bases swiftly, and field. Throwing the ball, that was the only element missing from his good all-round game.

Even though David more than held his own playing ball with his friends in sandlot games, Little League seemed out of the question. Someone suggested to David's mother, Brenda Stokes, that she enroll David in the Little League's Challenger Division for handicapped kids, but when she mentioned it to him, he wasn't interested.

"If he was going to play at all, he told me, he was going to play in the regular Little League," Brenda Stokes remembered her son saying. "His reasoning? He said he wasn't handicapped." Which is exactly the way David Potter has always felt, the loss of his two hands at the age of four notwithstanding. Still, even when he was eleven, David knew that if he went out for Little League some kids would make fun of him, even more so than had happened in the past. *So*, he thought to himself, *why not forget it. I know I'm good, and I know I can hit better than most kids my age,* he said to himself, *but I can't throw and I don't want to be made fun of. So who needs it?*

Little League is a big deal for most kids who like sports, especially when they're good athletes. For all of its attendant evils—its super-organization, adult control, and, at times, overwhelming pressures to do well—it is still the first big hurdle an aspiring ballplayer must face. Pickup games that are organized and played with friends may be far more fun— and in the long run a much more meaningful experience—but Little League, for better or for worse, is where the real competition is between the ages of nine and thirteen. The season, however, usually ends about the time school vacation starts, leaving many if not most kids to create their own fun and games in an era when overzealous adults have taken the creativity out of children's games, including baseball.

Mason Philpot, even at the age of eleven, knew a good ballplayer when he saw one. In his good friend David Potter, he saw a very good ballplayer indeed. So when David told Mason he was going to pass on playing Little League, Mason Philpot suddenly became an even better friend. "I knew he was a good athlete, and I knew he could play Little League and be good," Mason said before teaming up with David during the 1994 Pony League season. "So I told him I thought he should go out because I knew he could do well."

Two years after it happened, David Potter remembered the conversation vividly. "Mason really encouraged me to play. He said to me, 'You can do it, I know you can.' So I decided to try it. My mom told me they might not let me play in the regular Little League, and I said to her that if they don't, then I'll play in the Challenger Division. But after my talk with Mason, I really wanted to play in the regular Little League."

That's because David Potter never thought he was different than any other kid, even though he had no hands since his fateful accident on December 29, 1985, in Houston. That afternoon, David had gone out to play with some friends in the parking lot of the apartment complex where he lived with his mother.

"We had been walking past this transformer box a couple of days earlier, and I told David to stay away from it because I knew the kids were able to open it if they wanted to," Brenda Stokes said. "After a while, this girl, who was about thirteen, came to the door and told me that David had kind of gotten shocked. I didn't know what she meant at first, and she ran off. Then as I was getting ready to go outside, she came running back and said, 'He's kind of sleeping on the ground.' And then she ran off again. When I got out to the parking lot, David was lying on the ground, unconscious, and the other kids had all taken off. Then he started getting up and falling down. Somebody called an ambulance, and they took him to Herman Hospital. For three days they gave David blood transfusions and tried to save his hands, but they couldn't." Finally, on New Year's Day, 1986, eleven days before his fifth birthday, surgeons amputated both of David Potter's scorched hands a few inches below each elbow.

"At that point, his hands looked like snakeskin," Brenda Stokes recalled. "When I told David they were going to have to cut off his hands, he cried and said to me, 'Are they going to have to use a butcher knife, Mom?' It was very sad."

Through a long convalescence followed by extensive rehabilitation, little David Potter's spirits stayed high. "He never got down on himself or felt sorry for himself," his mother said. "Sometimes I'd be on the verge of tears because of what had happened, and he'd kind of sense it and say to me, 'Don't worry, Momma. I'm going to be okay, and I'll be able to do all the things the other kids do.' And before long he was out playing with his friends again, riding a bike and learning how to skateboard."

But the game he was just starting to play at the time of his accident, and the one he liked best, baseball, seemed out of the question. So when the 1986 baseball season came around and many of his friends began to play in the pee-wee leagues and on neighborhood sandlots, David watched longingly, yearning to play but bedeviled by a sense of hopelessness because of his devastating handicap. From time to time he'd put a glove on his left stump and, after a fashion, play catch with a friend—catching the ball and then, in effect, catapulting it back out of the glove in what for him had become his throwing motion.

"He'd keep telling me how much he wanted to play baseball because it was his favorite game," his mother said, "but I just didn't see how it would be possible. Then when David was six, we went out to Bear Creek Park one Sunday, and, at David's suggestion, we took along a ball, bat and glove. I thought that David just wanted me to hit some balls to him, but when we got there, he said, 'Mom, I want to learn how to bat, but I don't know how I'm going to do it.' I could tell he was very determined, so I started to try to show him different ways that I thought might work. Fortunately, I had been very active in sports, including softball, so I knew something about batting. Finally, I tucked the handle under his left armpit and put the shaft on his right stump and started lobbing in pitches to him. He had trouble at first, and I could see he was very frustrated, but we kept at it because he was so very determined. And eventually he started making contact even though he couldn't hit the ball very far. But I kind of feel that David realized right there and then that he was on the way. After that, we kept practicing, and before long he started playing ball with his friends, including Mason Philpot, who David met in the first grade after we moved and who soon became his best pal."

Despite his disability and his highly unusual hitting style, David soon developed into one of the best hitters in his age group in the Spring Branch section of Houston. And, equally as amazing, he was starting to emerge as a good shooter in basketball. "When we moved to our new house, David was just starting to get interested in basketball, so we put a hoop up on the garage. And he would go out and shoot for hours, flipping the ball up in a sideways motion with his arm stumps. So now, not only was he starting to play baseball, but he was starting to play basketball, too. Through it all, he never felt sorry for himself, although at times he would get angry when he couldn't do something like tie his shoes, which was just impossible. But I kept telling him right from the start after he came home from the hospital that he was going to have to learn how to do a lot of things all over again, and that he was going to have to try harder and harder, but that he could do it. And I could tell just by looking in his eyes that he was going to do it because he was so determined, especially when it came to sports."

By the time David Potter turned nine, he was as good an athlete as any other kid his age in Spring Branch. There was little he couldn't do. While he had trouble throwing a football, he could catch one, often spectacularly, by grasping the ball with his stumps or even with one stump. And, like his friends, he could ride a bike and a skateboard, swim, and even bowl. But one liability gnawed at him—he still could not throw a baseball. Little League was almost upon him and because of Mason Philpot's encouraging words, he was going to give it a try. And why not? He knew he could probably hit as well as anyone, he could certainly catch a baseball, and he was a fast man on the bases. Now if only he could throw.

Unsurprisingly, heads turned and some people even stared when David Potter showed up for tryouts during the first practice session of the Spring Branch National Little League in late February of 1992, when he was eleven years old. "When we got to the field, someone involved with the league said to me that maybe David should think of playing in the Challenger's Division, but I told him that he didn't consider himself handicapped," Brenda Stokes recollected.

David heard the conversation and, though it hardly surprised him, it made him even more determined to play in the regular Little League. "I knew I could do it; otherwise, I wouldn't have gone out."

It did not take long for coaches conducting the tryouts to see that David Potter, though he could not throw, did indeed belong. He caught every ball hit his way, both in the air and on the ground, and he amazed everyone with his batting prowess. Though he was unable to attend the first practice session, Ken Parsons, a coach and member of the league's board of directors, soon heard all about David Potter.

"When I asked Ray Johnson, the president of the league, how the practice went, he started raving about this new kid," Parsons said. "But then he said to me, 'But the kid has no hands.' And I said, 'So what. Half the kids at this level have no hands, meaning that they have trouble fielding. But then he said, 'Ken, you don't understand. This kid really has no hands; he's an amputee. Well, at that point my mouth dropped. 'And he wants to play regular Little League,' Ray went on. 'And, you know what, he can really hit.' Well, I was dumbfounded, and I thought to myself, this kid really has a lot of guts to do what he's doing. And of course I couldn't wait to see him play."

As it developed, Ken Parsons got to see David Potter play basketball before baseball and when he did, he was left virtually incredulous. "I knew David was a close friend of Mason Philpot's who our son, Joshua, also knew and whom I had coached." Parsons said. "So I called the Philpots, and Mason's mother, Meg, answered, and I asked about David. By chance, he was at the Philpots playing one-on-one basketball against Mason, and Meg suggested I drive over to see him, which I did. When I got there, they were going at it, and I couldn't believe my eyes. David was absolutely thrashing Mason. And not only could he shoot the basketball well, but he could run like a gazelle and jump like a jackrabbit. It was obvious that he was a very good athlete. After that, we talked, and he told me how much he wanted to play in our league."

If Ken Parsons was amazed at how well David Potter could play basketball without hands, he was in for an even bigger surprise when he first saw him on a baseball field. "When I saw him hit and field, I was absolutely astonished. He could do everything, and do it well, but it was just impossible for him to throw. But before I ever saw him play, I said to Joshua, who is a year younger than David and was also going to play in the league, 'We've got to help this kid in some way so that he can throw a baseball.' Joshua was working on a science project in school, in which everyone was supposed to come up with some kind of an invention. He was good at math and science and he had a good imagination, so I was kind of picking his brain, and I asked him, 'What can we do to help him throw the ball?'"

At that point, young Josh Parsons' creative juices began to flow. And given the science project he was about to embark on, the timing was perfect. Even more important, he thought, was a golden opportunity to help a kid his own age—a kid with a severe handicap who loved sports—to play baseball. "I think I'll be able to think of something, Dad," he said to his father as he turned and headed into the kitchen of their home. There, he rummaged through kitchen drawers and a pantry before coming across some paper cups. *Paper cups*, he thought to himself. *Now if I turn them around and put them bottom to bottom, I think I might have something.*

"Dad," Joshua called out to his father, "I think I've hit on something." In a matter of minutes, Josh Parsons was sitting down drawing a design of a throwing device he had envisioned after putting the two paper cups bottom to bottom in the kitchen. "If this works, Dad, I think David will be able to throw a baseball, and I think it's going to work, too."

Thoroughly absorbed by his idea, Josh Parsons then made a paper model in the shape of a scoop—the crux of his idea being that David Potter, after catching a ball with his glove, would then flip it into the scoop on his other hand and throw it, much like a jai-alai player does with a cesta. Eager to help his son complete the project, Ken Parsons' first priority was to get some leather with which to make the actual throwing device that would be based on his son's pattern. Then in a matter of hours one Saturday afternoon, father and son, working together in what had become a labor of love, cut up some of the leather, stitched the pieces together, and, closely adhering to Joshua's paper model, stitched the pieces into one unit. Both Ken Parsons and his son looked at the finished product with pride and admiration. "Dad, it's going to work," Joshua said, his face aglow. "I know it is."

Ken Parsons, proud of his son's creative accomplishment, put his arm around him and replied, "I think you're right, Josh. I think it's going to work. Let's go outside and try it out." Out in the backyard, Josh Parsons put the "throwing arm," as he called it, on his right hand and a regular baseball glove on his other hand. After catching several balls thrown to him by his father, Joshua flipped them into the throwing device and "threw" the balls back.

"It works, Dad! It works!," he cried out after the second throw. "Now we've got to let David try it out."

Suddenly it dawned on young Joshua Parsons. He hadn't even met the boy for whom he had just made an ingenious device that just might enable him to throw a baseball for the first time in his young life, but the time had now come. "We found out that David was at Mason Philpot's house, so we drove over," Ken Parsons said. "But we didn't tell him why we were coming. I'll never forget the expression on David's face when we showed him what Josh had made for him. And when we put it on and showed him how it was supposed to work, it was like a religious experience. Then we went across the street to a lot with some gloves and a ball. Josh Parsons, though, sensed some doubt in David's mind as to whether the device would actually work."

"I could tell that he was doubtful as we put it on his right hand," Josh said in recalling the experience. "So I said to him, 'David, it's going to help you throw; I know it is.'"

David Potter still looked at his new friend dubiously, though at the same time eager to try out the strange-shaped device. "I remember the first ball I threw to him," Ken Parsons said. "He caught it, flipped it into the throwing arm and zipped it right at me, real hard." As he did, Josh Parsons, beaming, yelled out, "Thataway, David. Good throw."

For about five minutes, Ken and Josh Parsons played catch with David. Not every one of his throws was on target like the first one; but Ken Parsons knew accuracy would come with time, and there was still plenty of time between now and the first game of the season. Another thing that Ken Parsons knew was that he wanted David Potter on his team with his son, Josh, and not just because Josh had made the throwing arm. He knew that in David Potter he would have a very good all-round ball player who could do it all, including throw. "I'll never forget the look on David's face when he made that first throw," Ken Parsons said. "And then later, as we were about to leave, he looked down at the throwing arm and said, 'Is it mine?' And I said, 'Of course, David. We made it especially for you.' And he said,

'You mean to keep forever?' Josh and I both smiled at that and then Josh said, 'Forever, David. Forever.'"

Two years later, in 1994, when he was thirteen, David Potter recalled how eager he was to show his mother the strange-looking throwing device that fit snugly over his right arm, held together by some Velcro strips. "It felt funny when I first put it on, and I really didn't think it was going to work," he said. "And I couldn't understand why Josh Parsons had made it for me because we didn't even know each other. So I thought it was kind of strange. But then when I started throwing with it, I really felt good, and I realized that maybe it would work after all."

Subsequently, Ken Parsons was able to draft David along with Mason Philpot for his team, the Mustangs, in the Spring Branch National Little League. Not all of David's teammates were thrilled at the prospect of having a boy with no hands on their team. "At first, some of them would say, 'You can't play. What are you doing here?'," David recalled. "And they'd make fun of me. But I wouldn't say anything."

That was before the season had even begun, though, and none of his teammates were making fun of David any more. "He hit the ball real good in practice, and he showed that he could not only catch, but that he could throw, too," Ken Parsons said. "He could catch fly balls better than any of my other outfielders, and, before long, he could throw it as far as any of them. He was definitely in the upper half of the talent on our team, and we had a very good team."

David Potter remembered how, once he had demonstrated his abilities, the attitudes of some of his teammates changed. "After I did well, some of the same kids who were making fun of me at first would come up and be friendly and say, 'Hi, David.' Which was okay with me."

But if David Potter's problems with some of his teammates had been cleared up, even bigger problems loomed with grownups in the Little League organization. "Some people felt that, because David had no hands, he belonged in the Challengers' Division," Ken Parsons said. "And I told David that right at the beginning after we drafted him. When I did, he said, 'Okay. If they don't let me play in the regular league, I'll play in the Challenger's.' That's the way he was; nothing seemed to bother him."

But opposition to David playing in the regular Little

League bothered Ken Parsons, even though it was based on technical grounds. In an effort to ensure that David would be cleared to play in the Spring Branch National Little League, Parsons sought out help from orthopedic specialists and a psychologist from the University of Houston. In each instance, he found not only a sympathetic ear but words of encouragement, both for himself and for David Potter. At Parsons' request, two orthopedic surgeons examined David and wrote letters saying he was physically capable of playing Little League baseball. So, too, did Dr. Charles Meisgeier, a professor in the Department of Educational Psychology at the University of Houston, who wrote, "It has been found that substantial benefits accrue to nonhandicapped individuals by observing a handicapped individual overcome obstinacies, persist in acquiring needed skills, and in learning to provide support for others." Copies of the letters were sent to the administrator for Little League baseball in Houston and later to the main Little League offices in Williamsport, Pennsylvania, along with a photo of David Potter wearing his throwing arm which, Parsons noted, enabled David to throw accurately for between twenty-five to thirty yards (as the 1992 season progressed, that accuracy range increased considerably). In his own cover letter to the national Little League headquarters, Ken Parsons, referring to David Potter, said: "His presence has been a rewarding experience for my little players, and David relishes being treated like 'one of the guys.' He's truly an amazing and special young man. And whatever decision is rendered, I, for one, have been enriched by knowing this boy."

Parson's letter-writing campaign paid off, albeit belatedly. It was aided in large measure by a widely-circulated Associated Press photo of David, in his Mustangs' uniform, tossing a ball with his new "throwing arms." "Although the season was already underway, we still hadn't received official approval from the national Little League headquarters in Williamsport," Parsons said. "But then after the picture of David hit the wires, reporters began calling up the Little League's main office to ask whether David was eligible to play in the regular Little League, and the Little League president, Con Hale, said that he was. As it was, we didn't receive official permission from the League's headquarters until July after the season had ended."

While his father was working hard to clear away the bureaucratic red tape that might jeopardize David Potter's status as a Little Leaguer, Josh Parsons was not only enjoying an outstanding season with the Mustangs, but also was given a special award by the Houston Inventors Association for "inventing" a throwing arm for his new friend. "Joshua's invention showed a tremendous amount of ingenuity," Chuck Mullen, chairman of the inventors' group, said. "And it's the kind of invention that has already had a positive impact." In addition, in late May of 1992, Joshua and David were notified by the National Easter Seal Society that they had been picked to receive the Society's first Friends Who Care Award, given "to a young person or persons whose actions have made a difference and enhanced another's independence." Later, in early August, Josh received a letter from Jim Abbott, the big-league pitcher, then with the California Angels, who was born without a right arm.

"Your efforts on behalf of David helped make a young man's dream come true," Abbott wrote. "Rather than experience such bitter disappointment because of the accident, your caring has allowed David to learn and understand that he can still compete and, more importantly, belong."

Despite appearances on several network television shows, along with a number of other distractions, both David Potter and Josh Parsons had excellent seasons. "It wasn't long before David was intimidating pitchers," Ken Parsons remembered. "He didn't hit for power, but he certainly did hit, and he had the knack of being able to put the ball in the hole between infielders." Early in the season, Parsons had one or even two infielders go out into short rightfield to cutoff his throws. But as the season progressed, and David's accuracy and strength with his throwing arm improved, that no longer was necessary. "By midseason, he could throw the ball as far as anybody," Parsons said. Playing rightfield, David, as noted earlier, finished the season with a .429 batting average, which is high in any level of competition, and a .733 on-base percentage. That on-base percentage was two points higher than Josh Parsons' .731. Josh's overall statistics were downright awesome: a .647 batting average, an .851 slugging percentage as the Mustangs' starting first-baseman, and a 3–0 record as the team's number two pitcher. Thanks in large part to David Potter's contributions, both at bat and in the field, the Mustangs won their divisional championship with a 15–2 record.

"It was a very talented team, and David was one of our best talents," Ken Parsons said. One of the highlights of the season for both David and Josh occurred on June 15 when they both were invited to throw out ceremonial first-pitches at an Astros game at the Houston Astrodome—Josh with his strong right arm and David with the throwing arm invented and made by his Mustangs teammate.

"It was a season that I certainly will never forget," Ken Parsons said with a smile. "And not just because we did so well. From the very beginning, there were so many distractions, and, yet, neither Josh nor David ever lost their focus. It was truly amazing. And it was great to see the way everybody—the kids, their parents, and just about everyone else—responded to David."

They responded about as well the following season when David, then a Little League veteran at the age of twelve, batted over .400 again while playing first base in Galveston, where his family had moved in October of 1992. First base was far more of a challenge than rightfield, since a first-baseman gets to handle the ball more often, and David wanted the challenge. By then, he was more accustomed to the throwing arm, and his accuracy had increased immeasurably. So, too, had his velocity and the distance that he could throw a baseball. In Galveston, he also played tackle on a Pop Warner football team and was the high scorer of his team in a Boys' Club basketball league. All the while, though, he missed his friends in Houston; thus he was ecstatic when his mother told him in October of 1993, that they were moving back to Houston, where once again, he could see his old friend Mason Philpot and the boy who had become his new friend—and a very special friend, at that—during the 1992 Little League season, Josh Parsons. They would no longer play Little League baseball together, since by 1994, David and Mason had turned thirteen, and Little League was behind them. But they all knew that somewhere down the road—in the Pony League, in Babe Ruth, or American Legion—they would meet again on the baseball field, either as teammates or as opponents. And, as young as they were, they would never forget that very special season of 1992.

Meanwhile, young Josh Parsons went on inventing things that would help other kids, such as a special infield training glove that forces a young player to use two hands in fielding a ground ball—it was displayed at the Houston Inventors Association convention in 1993—and a throwing arm similar to the one he devised for David. "A boy from Butte, Montana, named Zach Chatriand, who had lost both of his hands in an accident, had read about Josh and David and wrote a letter to Joshua," Ken Parsons said. "What he missed most of all, he said, was throwing snowballs with his friends. After we got his measurements, Josh went ahead and made a similar throwing device with a strap that went around the shoulder. The boy was absolutely delighted."

And very grateful. Perhaps as much as David Potter was when Josh Parsons, a boy whom he had not yet met, was so touched by his plight and his yearning to throw a baseball as well as any of the other kids in the Spring Branch National Little League in 1992.

"I'll never forget Josh doing what he did for me when we had never even met," David said after returning to Houston. "It meant I could play ball just like the other kids, and do just what they could do. And what made it great was that we turned out to be teammates and friends."

CHAPTER 5

DON WARDLOW

"We're looking at Luis Lopez as he steps to the plate," Don Wardlow, the radio color commentator for the New Britain Red Sox, said into his microphone in the tiny broadcast booth at Beehive Field. Maybe everyone else at the cozy ballpark in New Britain, Connecticut, was looking at the second baseman for the Canton-Akron Indians as he stepped into the batter's box; but not Don Wardlow, who has been blind since birth and likes to use such figures of speech.

What would seemingly be an insurmountable handicap in broadcasting a baseball game has not been a deterrent to Wardlow, believed to be the first blind play-by-play broadcaster ever. Like a promising young player, Wardlow had been making his way up the ladder in baseball's "bushes," having progressed from Class A to AA with his broadcast partner, Jim Lucas, who is also in his thirties. "We're paying our dues and getting plenty of experience right now," Wardlow said shortly before the 1994 season began. "And our goal is to make it to the big time—to the majors."

For a man who was born without eyes, and thus has no conception of what anything looks like, that would seem to be an unattainable goal. After all, Wardlow has never known the sight of faces, colors, or shapes. He has no idea what a ballpark, a baseball diamond, or even a bat, ball, or a glove, look like. But, as Wardlow will tell you, he need not know any of those things to broadcast a baseball game, not as long as he can rely on the senses he does possess—touch, smell, taste, and, most important of all, hearing. "As long as I can hear and smell and touch, I can do baseball," he said with his ever-present smile while his black Labrador seeing-

64

Damn the Disabilities

eye dog, Gizmo, lay stretched out at his feet.

As the youngest of five children whose four siblings are all sighted, Wardlow was raised to believe that he could do just about anything, so long as he put his mind to it. "We really didn't treat Don any differently than our other kids," his mother, Peg Wardlow, said at the family home in Woodbridge Township, New Jersey. "He went to public schools just like the other kids, and he had a lot of friends, who would come over and play with him. And his brothers and sisters rough-housed with him, especially our second youngest, Diane, who is four years older than Don. There was no quarter given. And, like the others, he was given chores to do, such as emptying out the dishwasher, putting out the garbage, and vacuuming. And in the summer, he had to do weeding in the garden. Early on, I taught Don the difference between the weeds and flowers, and he instinctively caught on because of his feel."

Even earlier, Wardlow became enchanted with baseball, via the radio. "As a little kid, I was crazy about country music, and still am," he said "I'd listen to it on a New York radio station. The same station carried the New York Mets games, and I became fascinated with baseball by listening to Bob Murphy, Lindsey Nelson, and Ralph Kiner. By the time I was eight, I was in love with baseball. After that my dad began taking me to some games, and I don't know how he did it, but eventually he arranged for me to meet with Murphy, Nelson, and Kiner at Shea Stadium. It was a huge thrill."

Having given birth to four healthy children, Peg Wardlow had no inkling that her fifth and last child would be born without eyes. "It's an extremely rare thing," she said. "My obstetrician told me that he had delivered thousands of babies, and Don was the first one born without eyes. But we accepted the fact, and so did Don from the very beginning. We told him when he was very young that 'God made you this way, and we just have to go forward.'"

Far from being embittered about his sightlessness, little Don Wardlow was a fun-loving extrovert, full of life. "Don had a great rapport with kids in elementary school, and a lot of them would come over and play with him," Peg Wardlow recalled. "In a way, I think they were excited about Don, particularly in the early grades, because he was blind. And they were all very protective of him. But then in junior high school it changed somewhat. Some kids would say, 'Hey, he's different.' And they would put things in his way and pull chairs out from under him. But he never complained about it. Then in high school, it got better."

It was also where, in a sense, Wardlow's broadcasting career began. "By then I was convinced I wanted to work in radio, probably as a deejay," Wardlow said. "While at JFK High in Iselin, New Jersey, I noticed that the morning announcements, which were done on the school PA system, were pretty bad. So I went to the office and volunteered to do them. I guess I did okay, because they let me do them for three years, including my puns and jokes." Wardlow has a penchant for puns. Following one particularly bad one, his broadcast partner, Jim "Tiny" Lucas, said on the air, "That's it. I'm out on strike. Let the blind guy do the play-by-play."

While in high school, Wardlow also manned the public address system for wrestling matches and basketball games. "That was easy, since all I did was introduce the lineups and, at the basketball games, give the score after each quarter. Once, though, the local radio station came to do a game and, I guess for better background, asked if I could do the game basket by basket. I did, with my dad at my side telling me who scored.

It was at Glassboro State College (now Rowan College) in New Jersey that Wardlow met Lucas and, as it turned out, established both a close friendship and a relationship as a baseball broadcasting team. "At first, I majored in partying and wasn't much of a student," Wardlow recalled. "But then when I realized I was on the verge of flunking out, I began to hit the books and got straight A's." Wardlow also signed on as a sportscaster on the campus radio station. "I was doing a five-minute 'scoreboard' show once a week, as were a number of other guys, including Tiny," he said. "And on November 15, 1983—I'll never forget the date—I was coming out of the studio after doing a show when I heard someone say, 'Hey, Don, nice job.' I knew right away it was Tiny, because I had heard him doing the scorecard show, and I knew he was in my algebra class. I also knew he was the last guy on my list of people to ask if they'd be willing to have me as a partner doing some Glassboro State games. Sixteen others had already said no. 'You're Jim Lucas,' I said. 'Are you up for a challenge? How'd you like to do play-by-play

It was the beginning of a beautiful friendship and one of the strangest pairings ever in sports. Wasting no time, Lucas and Wardlow asked the manager of the campus station if they could broadcast at least a couple of the school's men's varsity basketball games. "He told us to make a tape and then let him hear it," said Wardlow, who as a sophomore, was two years behind Lucas. "So we taped one of the games, and I guess he must of liked it because they then let us do several games." But that was basketball, and it merely provided Wardlow and Lucas an opportunity to work together as a broadcasting pair before switching over to their first sports love, baseball.

"I'll never forget our first baseball game, Glassboro against Temple on March 27, 1984, on the campus station. We were comfortable working together from the start, and we got some good feedback from kids on campus. So we kept going and did another three or four baseball games on the air and about the same number on tape, for our own benefit, mainly for the experience."

But then the partnership ended, at least temporarily, in May when Lucas graduated and took a job with a collection agency. "Not exactly what I had in mind while I was at Glassboro, but the best thing I could get at the time" said Lucas, who is also from New Jersey. "Meanwhile, Don and I vowed to stay in close touch." But the chances of that happening, and of Wardlow and Lucas being reunited as a baseball broadcast team, grew even more remote when Lucas got married in 1986 and moved to Middletown, Connecticut. Wardlow, in the meantime, continued broadcasting baseball with several different partners during his final two years at Glassboro State. Following graduation in December of 1986, he spent nine months as an employment counselor and three years as a quality control checker for Recording for the Blind in Princeton, New Jersey. All the while, he nurtured the dream of being reunited with Lucas and launching a career as partners doing professional baseball and, who knows, maybe even going as far as the majors. To keep sharp, he kept doing taped versions of college baseball and football games, and some boxing cards in Philadelphia and New York.

"I'd usually be able to line up a partner, quite often by

approaching a college sports information director," Wardlow recollected. "Once, when I wanted to tape a Rutgers game, I asked the Rutgers coach if he could spare anyone, and Bobby McDonald, who went on to become a big league pitcher, volunteered to do the play-by-play, since he wasn't pitching that day. Trouble is, Bobby chewed tobacco, and that's not the best thing to do when you're doing play-by-play. If I couldn't get anyone to work with me and the game was being broadcast, I'd listen to the broadcast on a headset and do my own recreation. If nothing else, it was good experience."

By 1988, Wardlow and Lucas, who as promised had stayed in close touch with one another, had been reunited on a part-time basis while keeping their day jobs. Equipped with microphones, tape recorders, headsets, a Braille typewriter, and yards and yards of wire and cord, Wardlow and Lucas began to broadcast big league games for an audience of two—themselves. Over a three-year period, after paying for their seats, they "broadcast" approximately 125 games from perches in the grandstand and bleachers at Yankee and Shea stadiums in New York, at Veterans Memorial Stadium in Philadelphia, Fenway Park in Boston, and Three Rivers Stadium in Pittsburgh. "I also did four games by myself at the Metrodome in Minneapolis while I was on vacation in July of 1990," Wardlow recalled. Doing color commentary when you can't see sounds tough enough, but a blind man doing play-by-play of a game without a partner? "It was actually pretty easy," Wardlow said with a sly smile. "I'd listen to Herb Careal and John Gordon doing the Twins' games on my radio headset and instantly do my own version on my tape recorder."

There was a definite method to this madness, which amused but did not bother nearby fans, Lucas recalled. "Some of them would look at us kind of strange, and I can't say I blame them," Lucas said. "But the only problem we ever had was when a fan dropped a roast beef sandwich and Gizmo [Wardlow's seeing-eye dog] ate it in one gulp. As for the games, we were doing them for two reasons—to get some experience and to build up a resume. At the same time, Don and I, as always, had a lot of fun." But Wardlow had his doubts, and Lucas could discern them, as to whether he, as a blind man, could really make it as a baseball broadcaster. "At times I could tell that Don just couldn't believe that he could do it, and I'd say to him, 'You're good, Don, believe me; you're really good.'"

Meanwhile, the game tapes began to accumulate, heard only by Wardlow and Lucas, who critiqued themselves mercilessly, and some friends and family members. "We called what we were doing 'The Basement Network' because we felt that some day, if we didn't make it, all these game tapes would wind up in someone's basement in the years to come, Lucas said." "But meantime, even though no one was listening, we did every game like it was the seventh game of the World Series."

Finally in March of 1990, the unlikely broadcasting team of Wardlow and Lucas made its move, figuratively speaking, when they sent a tape of a Yankee-Brewer game they had broadcast on July 1, 1989, to 176 professional baseball teams—"every single one that we were aware of," Lucas said. "Forty-four responded, and forty-three of them were rejections." But, fortunately for 'The Basement Network,' the forty-fourth response was from Mike Veeck, the son of the late baseball owner-showman Bill Veeck, who like his father knows a good gimmick when he sees or hears one. (Veeck's father, as the owner of the old St. Louis Browns, was the man who signed midget Eddie Gaedel to a one-game contract and sent him to bat as a pinch-hitter—he drew a walk.) The younger Veeck, the general manager and part-owner of the Miracle of the Class A Florida State League, not only wrote back but invited Wardlow and Lucas to come on down to Pompano Beach, Florida, for a game audition on July 2, 1990. A chip off the old block, Veeck does not deny that he had an ulterior motive.

"I'd be lying if I didn't say I thought we could get some mileage out of this as a promotion," he said. "But by the third inning, I knew Jim and Don were really good and that I was going to hire them."

During their first season, in 1991, Wardlow and Lucas broadcast fifty-one games while the Miracle was based in Pompano Beach. The following year, when the club moved to Fort Myers, they did all 140 of the Miracle games. "At the end of the season I told Jim, 'You've got to leave,'" Veeck recalled. "Jim looked at me, and I could see he was annoyed and upset. But then I told him that he and Don had done everything they could do at our level and that it was time for them to move up."

Lucas and Wardlow heeded Veeck's advice. "Double-A was the next logical step, so I checked every Double-A team in the country and found that New Britain was the only one that didn't have a radio outlet," Lucas said. "Then I made our pitch to Gerry Berthiaume (the general manager of the New Britain Red Sox)—that we ourselves would buy the radio time, and all it would cost the club was two seats on the bus and a hotel room on the road. Gerry and his boss, Joe Buzas, who owns the club, then agreed to give us the broadcast rights, and then we bought time for all 140 games from WBIS in Bristol. Then Don and I spent the following winter selling all thirty-six hours of commercial time, along with Chick Minka [a longtime friend of Lucas', with a background in public relations and marketing, who works fulltime with Lucas and Wardlow, and thus along with Gizmo, is part of The Basement Network team]."

If Lucas serves as Wardlow's "eyes" in the broadcast booth, Wardlow reciprocates with a plethora of statistics and anecdotal information between pitches and innings, along with occasionally leading fans at Beehive Field in a seventh-inning rendition of "Take Me Out to the Ball Game" in a pleasant tenor voice. "Boo Moore has had a problem with Ks," Wardlow says in his relatively high-pitched but pleasing voice in referring to a New Britain hitter who is at bat in a game against Canton-Akron. "He had 107 last season at Lynchburg and 135 the year before. But he hits for power. Last year he had sixteen doubles, three triples, nineteen home runs and fifty ribbies [runs batted in]."

Those statistics come from one of a stack of Braille sheets in Wardlow's lap, which he leafs through constantly during a game. Most of them are prepared in advance while others, including his scoring of the game, are produced from inning to inning on a Braille typewriter. "Shane grounded to short his first time up," Wardlow says seizing a verbal cue from Lucas and referring to batter Shane Andrews of the Harrisburg Senators during another game after checking with his Braille scorecard. Before Andrews strikes out on a two-two pitch, Wardlow has told his listeners that Andrews' given name is Daryl ("but Shane is what he likes to be called"), is a .230 hitter who hit twenty-five home runs the previous season, is six feet one and 210 pounds, and "comes from a desolate part of the west—Carlsbad, New Mexico." This, mind you, is about a rival player. In talking about the New Britain Red Sox, Wardlow is apt to proffer everything from a player's favorite food to his shoe size.

"Don is Mr. Preparation," says Lucas who spent five years working for a collection agency before embarking on a baseball broadcasting career with Wardlow, which is now a full-time job. "He spends hours and hours preparing for each game, and he doesn't miss a thing."

Both during their days with The Basement Network and their two seasons with the Miracle in Florida, Wardlow had to rely for information on Lucas who would read him newspapers, statistics, and other material. Wardlow in turn would "Braille" into his Braille typewriter whatever he thought was relevant to the upcoming broadcast. As a time-saver, before their first season at New Britain, they bought a machine called "The Reading Edge," manufactured by Xerox Imaging Systems, which audibly reads out printed matter that is fed into it. "For the first time in his life, Don was able to 'read' his own mail," Lucas says. "And you should see his face light up when he does."

Given his unabashed love for baseball, it's not surprising that his face also lights up as he listens to stats and other data which he quickly transfers into Braille. When he's not transcribing statistics into "The Reader's Edge," Wardlow may be listening to his vast collection of old baseball tapes, dating from the early 1930s, snippets of which he incorporates into his broadcasts. Not surprisingly, Wardlow's idols are not old-time players, but past and present broadcasters, like Red Barber, Mel Allen, Bob Murphy, Jack Buck, Frank Messer, Jack Brickhouse, Ned Martin, Chuck Thompson, John Gordon, and Andy Musser. On road trips Wardlow usually curls up in his seat on the team bus, puts on his headset, and listens to tapes of old times, both for pleasure and for possible use on the air. When the Britsox, as they are often referred to in the New Britain area, are at home, Wardlow also spends considerable time listening to old tapes and "watching," to use his own term, games on television with Lucas and Minka, with whom he shares a house. In the off season most of his day is spent on the phone, trying to persuade potential advertisers to buy time on Britsox broadcasts, which were shifted to a bigger-watt station in Middletown during their second season in Double-A.

"Don's a good salesman," says Lucas. "He's very persuasive and doesn't give up easily." Lucas and Minka also spend most of their off season selling time for their broadcasts on station WGNX.

Though Wardlow can't see what's happening during a game, he can feel and his touch is an integral part of his work as a baseball commentator. For instance, before each game Wardlow, accompanied by Gizmo, goes through a ritual that includes a visit to home plate and the pitcher's mound, a walk around the bases, and, during his first trip to a ballpark, a journey to the outfield to touch and feel the fences. "That all gives me a better feel for the game," Wardlow says. He then does his pregame show and heads for the press box with Giz," as he calls his canine companion. "I don't know how you do it, going up all those steps," Lucas said to him during a game in New Britain. "It's easy," Wardlow replied with a smile. "Just one step at a time."

Occasionally, Lucas lets Wardlow describe some of the action. "Don will be in the middle of a story as a pitch comes in," Lucas said. "And I'll tell him in headset, without it going on the air, that so-and-so has flied to center. And he'll stop his story and say, 'There's a high one to center, Jim Morrison waits for it and makes the catch for the second out.' And then he'll resume his story without missing a beat. Meanwhile, listeners are thinking, 'Hey, that's the blind guy that made that call. How'd he do that?'"

Not that Wardlow always has to be told what is happening, or what has happened. "The highlight of my career are two homers that I called while we were with the Miracle," he said, again with a smile. "I knew they were gone by the crack of the bat, although Tiny did help out."

To Wardlow, who has an impish sense of humor—he even loves blind jokes—being blind has advantages. "For one thing, I don't know who's white and who's black, not that it matters," he said. And at times his blindness leads to particularly incisive questions. After Harrisburg outfielder Curtis Pride hit a foul dribbler in front of the plate one day, Wardlow asked, "How does Curtis know it's foul, Jim? He's deaf." Lucas responded by telling his partner that the umpire, aware of Pride's deafness, had signaled the ball foul. "Oh, I see," replied Wardlow. "That certainly makes sense."

So do Lucas and Wardlow as a team. One thing is for

sure: there is never any dead air when they're doing a game. The chatter is constant, interesting, and fun, and the timing is flawless. "Initially, I talked more than I wanted to, but that was because I included an awful lot of detail for Don's benefit. But now I use even more—the players' numbers, the color of their bats and batting gloves, and so on; but I think it's stuff that's of interest to the listener. Subconsciously, I guess I still say things that are aimed at Don, but not as much as in the past because I've come to realize he doesn't need to know a whole lot of extraneous details."

Wardlow's reaction? "Tiny is great with his description of what's happening; he certainly lets me know all that I need to know. But our roles are well-defined. I certainly can't perform his job, and he doesn't intrude on mine, which consists mainly of providing statistical and biographical background, and telling my stories."

At times Wardlow's blindness becomes lost on Lucas during a game. "The fact that Don can't see doesn't make him any less of a baseball announcer because he's so good at what he does," Lucas points out. "I know that when he gives it up, Don is going to want to be remembered as a good baseball broadcaster who just happened to be blind."

And just because he's blind doesn't mean that Don Wardlow can't go out on the field and find out just what it's like to be a ballplayer. Before one game at Beehive Field in New Britain, he donned the catcher's paraphernalia and went into a crouch, pounding the glove as catchers are wont to do. "I wanted to find out, first-hand, what it's like to be behind the plate," he said later. "And it was fun, although the mask is a lot heavier than I thought." Another time, wearing a New Britain Red Sox batting helmet, he stepped into the batting cage to take some swings for the first time. "I made contact, too—about four times," he said elatedly. On how many swings? "Oh I guess about forty," he responded with a self-deprecating laugh, something he does often. "But I did it. I hit the ball. What a great feeling."

On another occasion, Wardlow went down on the field at Memorial Stadium in Baltimore, where the Bowie, Maryland Baysox played their home games in 1993 while their own ballpark was being built. There he took his stance in the batter's box, facing an imaginary pitcher—perhaps Jim Palmer or Mike Cuellar. "What a thrill that was," he said animatedly at the remembrance, "especially since I saw my first World Series game at Memorial Stadium—the Pirates against the Orioles in 1971." Saw? "Sure, I saw it," he said by way of explanation. "It was the first World Series game I 'saw' on television. So I guess I saw the game in my own way."

Maybe, in truth, Wardlow doesn't actually see the game he loves with such unbridled passion. But he certainly hears it— the roar of the crowd, the crack of the bat, the popping of the ball into a glove. That's more than good enough for Don Wardlow, who hasn't found blindness to be a deterrent in broadcasting a game he has never seen played and never will.

CHAPTER 6

LARRY ALFORD

Having been a football star at Texas Tech University in the 1960s, it was understandable that Larry Alford would have liked his son, Larry, Jr., to follow in his footsteps on the gridiron. To a degree, young Larry did, starring in junior high school and as a freshman linebacker at McCullough High in The Woodlands, just outside of Houston. Like his dad, Larry, Jr., was an all-round athlete, excelling not only in football, but in baseball, basketball, soccer, and golf. "Golf was Larry's best sport, and had been since he was about eleven or twelve," Larry Alford, Sr., said in March of 1994. "But he wanted to play all sports, rather than just concentrate on golf, and he intended to be very good at it."

By the time Larry, Jr., was six years old, he was already hitting a golf ball well under the tutelage of his father at The Woodlands Country Club, where Alford, Sr., was a member. At ten he was taking part in junior tournaments in the Houston area, and by the time he was twelve, young Larry Alford had already accumulated a number of trophies which attested to his golfing skills. "By then, I knew Larry had it," his father, who himself had been an all-round athlete, said. "Not only did he have the physical tools, but he had the mental game, too. And a lot of the kids he was playing against were playing golf all year round, while Larry was still into all of his other sports. But I think his involvement in those sports helped him toughen his mental game."

About to begin his sophomore year at McCullough High, Larry, Jr., felt he had to make a decision. He knew that the varsity football coach wanted his players to focus on football in the spring, during spring practice, as well as during the fall. But to Larry, that would mean foregoing golf, which by the time he reached high school, was definitely not only his best sport, but his first love, too. "Gee, Dad, I really want to play golf all year-round, much as I like football," he said to his father in late August just before summer football practice sessions were to begin at McCullough High. "You won't be mad if I don't play football, will you?"

Larry, Sr., knew it was coming, so his son's decision hardly came as a surprise. He also knew that, at five-feet, five inches and 150 pounds, Larry, Jr., as good as he was, did not have too much future as a linebacker. "Of course not, Larry," Larry, Sr., replied. "I want you to do exactly what you want to do, and if it's play golf all the time, that's fine."

It was not fine, though, with the McCullough High varsity coach who was looking forward to having him on the team after his outstanding season with the freshman squad. "He was really ticked," Larry, Sr., recalled. "He wanted Larry on the team. But there was no way Larry was going to change his mind."

With far more time to devote to golf, Larry's game sharpened immeasurably. So much so that on a very competitive McCullough High School golf team, he was elected the most valuable player during both his sophomore and junior years when he shot in the mid-seventies. "No one works harder or is more unselfish than Larry," his high school coach, Danny Ihrig, once told Larry, Sr. "With Larry, the team always comes first."

Actually, golf, and his high school team came second, behind his family. His parents had divorced when he was ten, but Larry, Jr., though living at home with his mother and older sister, Kristi, remained close to his father. With Kristi attending Texas Tech while Larry was in high school, their mother, Missy, struggled to make ends meet by teaching art full time at a Houston school and, making and selling decorative wreaths and doing some wallpaper hanging on the side. To help ease the family's financial burden, Larry worked summers at the golf cart barn at The Woodlands Country Club and then at night waded into water hazards at Houston area golf courses with one of his best friends, Brendan Donley, to retrieve golf balls.

"We'd salvage as many as two-thousand a night and then sell them for eighteen cents a piece," Larry recalled. Money from those sales enabled Larry to play more and more golf, while his paychecks from his golfing job went to his mother, whom he also helped on her wallpaper hanging job.

Some years earlier, Larry had been touched by tragedy for the first time in his young life. From the time he was about three years old, his best pal had been Ryan Vanlandingham who lived two houses down the street in The Woodlands. Virtually inseparable, they played together on the same sports teams, rode side-by-side on their bikes, hung out at each other's homes, and sat together on the school bus each morning and afternoon.

"Ryan liked to do all the things I did, and we always did them together," Larry said. "The only exception was golf; he played a little, but nowhere near as much as I."

As full of life as his closest friend, Larry Alford, and seemingly as healthy, Ryan Vanlandingham appeared to have the whole world in front of him. But suddenly in October of 1985, when the boys were both twelve, a swelling inexplicably appeared on Ryan's jaw. Doctors determined that it was Burkitt's lymphoma, a rare form of cancer. Radiation and other treatments, including a bone marrow transplant failed to work. Even as his condition progressively worsened, Ryan's spirits remained high. Visiting his best friend almost daily, Larry Alford never once heard him complain about the pain he was enduring. Cheerful and smiling to the very end, Ryan died on July 27, 1986, only three months after he had been diagnosed with lymphoma. For young Larry, his best pal's long suffering and eventual death were devastating. *How could this happen to Ryan?* he asked himself. *How unfair this is.*

Now, five years after his best friend's death, Larry Alford was establishing himself as one of the best young golfers in the nation. Between his sophomore and senior years at McCullough High, he had done well playing in a number of national tournaments organized by the American Junior Golf Association. So well, in fact, that many college golf coaches had begun to pay close attention. More and more of them paid even closer attention in late June of 1991, following Alford's junior year, at the Mission Hills Desert Junior tournament in Rancho Mirage, California. Matched against seventy-four of the country's best junior golfers, Alford was tied for the lead going into the final round after shooting a seventy-two and a seventy-one. But during the last day, the friendly, outgoing teenager from The Woodlands slipped to a seventy-eight, which tied him for second place, five strokes behind the winner, Tiger Woods—now a member of the PGA circuit. That performance by Alford, who was ranked fifteenth among American junior golfers in 1991, drew the interest of coaches from some of the best college teams in the country, including those at Arizona, Arizona State, Stanford, and Oklahoma State. But the scholarship offer that interested him the most was one from virtually his own backyard—the University of Houston.

Arriving home, he told his mother about the offer, and his decision to accept it. "Mom, isn't this great?" he said excitedly. "Just think. Everything will be taken care of, and I'll be close to home, and it won't cost you anything while I'm going to college. And I'll be playing with one of the best college teams in the country." Missy Alford, fighting back tears, hugged her son tightly, knowing that he had worked so hard to earn a golf scholarship to make it easier for her.

Before formally accepting the Houston scholarship offer, Larry received a score of scholarship inquiries from schools with top college golf teams. Meanwhile, he practiced harder than ever, determined not only to do well during his final season at McCullough High and as a college golfer, but eventually to make it to the PGA tour. Another thing that did not change: on most nights, he and Brendan Donley, armed with rakes, continued to scour ponds and creeks at Houston area golf courses for errantly-hit golf balls, then cleaning and selling them for eighteen cents each.

"That's Larry. Finishing second in the biggest junior tournament of the year and then wading into water hazards to fish out golf balls," Larry Alford, Sr., said. "In no way was success going to change him."

Later that summer, on August 30, shortly after Larry had begun his senior year, a golf teammate asked if he could do him a favor and drive the teammate's father's Corvette to a relative's house. The teammate, in turn, would follow in his car and then give Larry a ride home. Larry said, "fine." Shortly after 6:00 P.M. Larry was driving the Corvette along Interstate 45, with his teammate following, when he lost control of the car. Swerving off I-45, the Corvette flipped over three times, catapulting Alford through the open sun roof and onto the roadway. Alford's friend, stunned and shaken, braked his car to a halt and saw his teammate lying motionless and bleeding badly from the head, face, and left arm. A number of other vehicles also stopped, but the occupants could do little for the motionless teenager, apart from trying to stop the bleeding until an ambulance arrived. Informed of the apparent severity of Alford's injuries, officials at Hermann Hospital dispatched its Life Flight helicopter, but shortly after taking off, the chopper ran into an electrical storm and was forced to turn back. An ambulance then was sent to the scene.

While the drama was unfolding, Missy Alford and a longtime friend, Jay Hall, a psychologist, were arriving at The Woodlands Pavilion with the parents of young Larry's boyhood pal, Ryan Vanlandingham, and another couple to attend a concert by singer Johnny Mathis. Shortly before the concert was to start, a friend, spotting Hall in the rear of the Pavilion with Paul Vanlandingham, hurried over excitedly and said, "Larry's been in an accident and is on is way to the hospital." Hermann Hospital, unable to reach Missy Alford, had phoned her brother, who, aware that she and Hall had gone to the Mathis concert, in turn called The Woodlands Pavilion. Somehow, the message reached the friend before it got to Missy Alford.

"All the friend could tell us was that Larry had hurt his eye and his hand," she recalled.

In a matter of minutes, Missy Alford, Jay Hall, and the Vanlandinghams were in Hall's car racing to Hermann Hospital, with the third couple following.

"I don't know how, but we got there before the ambulance," Missy Alford said. "Maybe it was because the ambulance hadn't gone to the scene until after the Life Flight helicopter had to turn back because of the storm. Larry's dad and a cousin also were there, and all of us waited anxiously in the emergency room, praying. Then we heard an ambulance pull up, and Big Larry and I both ran outside, just as they were starting to wheel Larry in. If they hadn't told me, I wouldn't have known it was Larry—his head was as big as a basketball."

Missy Alford, unprepared for what she had seen, blanched at the sight of her critically injured son, while Hall and the

Vanlandinghams looked on in shock as emergency medical personnel swiftly brushed past them with young Alford.

Moments later, a doctor emerged from behind a curtain and gestured for Missy Alford and Larry's father to come in. "Look at your son," the doctor said to Missy. *Oh my God!* she said to herself. *He's the color of gray ice!* Out of the corner of one eye, she saw what she perceived to be a look of horror on the face of one doctor.

"No one said anything at that point," Missy Alford recollected. "But I got the feeling that they wanted me to see Larry once more, maybe for the last time." To herself, Missy Alford pleaded, *Dear God, please save him.* Then as they were ushered out of the area, Missy cried out, "Larry! Larry! We love you."

In the emergency room they encountered their daughter, Kristi, who had just arrived at the hospital, hysterical. "Mom! Dad! Oh my God!," she shrieked. "What happened to Larry?"

Through the night, while doctors and nurses tended to young Larry Alford, Missy Alford, her former husband, their daughter Kristi, Jay Hall, the Vanlandinghams, and a few other relatives and friends waited anxiously, praying and periodically asking for word about Larry, but none was forthcoming. Finally, just before dawn, Dr. John Burns, an orthopedic surgeon, and another doctor appeared, looking somber.

"Both of them had frowns on their faces," Missy Alford was to recall two-and-a-half years later. "We didn't know what to expect."

From the moment Larry Alford arrived at Hermann Hospital, Dr. James "Red" Duke, the hospital's chief trauma surgeon, needed only a cursory look to discern the critical nature of his injuries. One thing was certain; young Alford's virtually severed left arm could not be saved. Far more important was a life-threatening head injury. And then there were the lesser, but still severe, injuries—a fractured eye orbital bone that had jarred Larry's left eye partially out of its socket; a broken jaw, ankle and shoulder blade; a collapsed lung; and a badly injured right arm.

"I remember shortly after Larry got to the hospital one of the doctors—it may have been Dr. Duke—told me, 'I don't think he's going to make it,'" Larry Alford, Sr., said. "He told me about the extent of the injuries and the seriousness of the head injury. And I could tell from what the doctor said that the arm wasn't going to be there anymore. But at that point I couldn't care less about the arm."

Now Larry Alford's parents, their daughter, Kristi, and the others all looked up at Dr. Burns and the second doctor. "I'm sorry but we had to amputate your son's left arm below the elbow," Dr. Burns said softly.

"Is he going to be all right?" Missy Alford asked.

"We don't know," Dr. Burns answered.

Like her former husband, Missy was unconcerned about her son's arm. "I just want Larry to live," she said to the doctors. "That's all I care about." Dr. Burns then recited a litany of injuries, stressing that Larry's condition was critical and that the outlook was unknown. Standing alongside Missy, Jay Hall, while well aware that the Alfords' main concern was their son's life, could not help but wonder about Larry's reaction to the loss of his left arm if he were indeed to survive. *How would Larry ever get along without golf?* he thought to himself of the teenager he had known since Larry was about five. But then, catching himself in mid-thought, Hall also realized that there was a far more pressing matter than a golf career at stake. *They've got to save Larry's life*, he said to himself. *That's all that matters right now.*

Finally, Dr. Burns said, "I know you've all been here a long time. Why don't you go home now and try to get some rest. And we'll do the best that we can."

For almost ten days Larry Alford, Jr., remained unconscious and in critical condition. Throughout that period, his parents alternated sitting at his side around the clock. Kristi joined in the vigil, as did Jay Hall and Larry, Sr.'s, second wife, Kay. Early one afternoon, while "Big Larry," as Missy Alford called her former husband, was at their son's side, doctors told him that it appeared that would have to amputate his right arm, too.

"It had puffed up like a basketball," Larry, Sr., said. Stunned by the development, he immediately telephoned Missy.

"I couldn't believe it," she said. In minutes she was en route to Hermann Hospital with Jay Hall. By the time she arrived, doctors had decided they could save the arm. "They told me they were within a few minutes of amputating it," Larry Alford, Sr., said.

About a week later, Larry, Sr., suddenly sensed some

movement in his comatose son. For the first time since the accident, his eyes opened momentarily, staring directly at the ceiling overhead.

"If you hear me, squeeze my fingers," his father, beside himself with joy, called out. Holding his son's right hand, Alford felt a slight tug. "He did it! He did it!" he yelled out. "Larry heard me." Many months later, Larry Alford, Sr., was to say, "I felt at that moment, for the first time, that Larry was going to make it, that he was going to come back to us. And he did, miraculously."

But both Larry and Missy Alford knew that, even assuming their son made a full recovery, extremely difficult days lay ahead. For one thing, young Larry eventually would learn that he had lost his left hand. In an effort to prepare him for the shock, they mentioned amputation often at his bedside, but groggy from medication, he was unable to comprehend. Still they knew that, inevitably, he would find out, and they hoped that one or the other would be with Larry when he did. By the time young Larry found out, the Alfords, though they spent hours with him every day, no longer were maintaining a round-the-clock vigil, since he was out of danger and recovering.

It happened in late September, almost a month after the accident. Awakening in the middle of the night at Hermann Hospital, Larry suddenly realized that his left hand was missing. Incredulous, he called for a nurse.

"I'm sorry, Larry," she said softly, "but they had to amputate your hand."

Stunned and not wanting to believe what he had been told, he replied, "I don't believe you. Call my daddy right away. He'll tell me the truth."

At about 4:30 in the morning, the nurse put through a call to Larry Alford, Sr. "You've got to come to the hospital right away," she said. "I tried to explain to your son that he lost his arm, but he doesn't believe me. And he's yelling for you."

Rushing to the hospital, Larry, Sr., hurried into his son's room and found him wide awake, staring at the ceiling. "Dad, they told me that my arm isn't there anymore," he mumbled through wiring which still kept his badly injured jaw shut.

"Son, it's not," Larry, Sr., replied, fighting back tears. "You were in a car accident, and they had to amputate."

They hugged one another as tears streamed down their faces.

"Dad, how am I going to play golf?" young Larry asked.

"You're going to play Larry. You're going to play. And you'll be fine," Larry, Sr., said.

Shortly thereafter, Larry was transferred to the Del Oro Institute for Rehabilitation in Houston. It was there, one night, that the impact of what had happened hit young Larry Alford with full force. "All of a sudden, it just hit me," he recalled. "I said to myself, 'How could you do something so stupid?' And then I had a grieving moment, and, after that, a long talk with the Lord. I realized that God had blessed me and had saved my life. And I told myself right then and there that nothing was going to stop me, and that I was going to play golf again and play it well."

Still, young Larry endured some dark moments, becoming furious at himself occasionally for what, in effect, he had done to himself. Most distressing of all was the realization that his dream of a golf scholarship to college and a career as a professional golfer had been shattered. But then one night, as he lay in bed lamenting his fate, he suddenly thought of his best childhood friend, Ryan Vanlandingham, and how he had so gallantly and cheerfully battled cancer without a complaint right up until his death at the age of twelve. *Look what happened to Ryan and how he handled it when he was only twelve years old,* he said to himself. *Who am I to feel sorry for myself after what he went through without complaining?* Right then, Larry vowed he would never feel sorry for himself. There would be no self-pity, and he would pursue his dream as a golfer.

Thereafter, the conversation often turned to golf when Larry, Sr., and Missy, and Jay Hall, a good club golfer, visited Larry, Jr., at the rehab center. "Not once did I ever see Larry depressed after the accident," Missy said. "He told me once, 'Mom, I did it to myself, so I'm to blame. And God saved my life. So I'm lucky.'"

Then one day in late September, while talking golf, Larry turned to his father and said, "Dad, do you have my clubs with you?"

Larry Alford was prepared for the moment. "Yeah, I've got them out in the trunk."

Beaming, young Larry then said, "Good. Can you get my pitching wedge. Maybe we can chip some balls outside." In minutes, young Larry, by then up and about for two weeks, and his father were on the way out to the lawn alongside the Del Oro Institute. Larry, Sr., dropped about a dozen balls and Larry, Jr., though he had lost forty pounds and was still weak, began to chip with his right arm. Ball after ball went soaring in beautiful arcs as both father and son looked on in delight.

"Dad, will you look at those shots," Larry, Jr., said, ecstatic at swinging a golf club again.

"You're doing great, son, just great," Larry, Sr., said.

A few days later, father and son, again unbeknownst to doctors and nurses, went outside to the lawn alongside the hospital. This time, Larry, Sr., brought along the seven and nine irons. Again, swinging rhythmically with his right arm, young Larry sent his shots high and straight ahead. The shots did not go anywhere near as far as he had hit them before the accident, but both the seven and nine are relatively "short irons," not intended for any great distance, but more for accuracy. Larry, Jr.'s, shots with the two clubs were on high arcs and down the middle.

Later, as they walked back toward the hospital, he asked his father, "Dad, do you think I'm going to be able to play again?"

Larry, Sr., stopped, turned to his son and said, "You've got a great challenge in front of you, Larry. But I know you can do it. It's entirely up to you."

Encouraged by his father's words, Larry, Jr., replied, "Dad, I know I can do it, too." After that, young Larry spent much of his time at the Del Oro Institute putting and chipping golf balls on a putting surface his father had put down in his room at the rehabilitation facility. Inevitably, the urge to get out onto a golf course began to develop stronger and stronger.

Larry, Sr., knew what was coming next, and in late October, while Larry, Jr., was still at the rehabilitation center, it happened.

"Dad, what do you say we go out to the course and play on a weekday?" he said to his father. A few days later, they were playing on the west course at The Woodlands Country Club, one of the club's four courses. Though he was still weak and lacking in stamina, Larry hit virtually all of his shots cleanly and accurately during his first outing as a one-handed golfer. His chipping and putting in particular were superb.

"Boy, Dad, this is great," he said at one point as he and

his father walked along a fairway.

"It sure is, Larry, and you're doing just fine." Fine indeed. By the end of eighteen holes, Larry, Jr., had shot an eighty-six, about ten strokes above his average before the accident, but an extraordinary score for a one-handed golfer, particularly on his first time out.

As they left the eighteenth green and headed for the clubhouse, young Larry turned to his dad and said, "Dad, do you think that I can still make it to the PGA tour?"

Larry, Sr., was prepared for that question, too. "Yes, I do," he replied. "But I think we're going to have to take this one day at a time."

More than two years later, Alford marveled at how well his son accepted his frightening misfortune. "There were only about two times where I can recall he was in a down mood," he said. "And when it happened it lasted maybe five minutes at a time. A couple of times he cried in my arms, but then I'd try to comfort him the best I could, and in a few minutes he would be fine. Once, after he'd been down, he said to me, 'Dad, I'm going to overcome this and be the first player on the PGA tour with one arm.'"

Shortly before young Larry went home from the Del Oro Institute, Missy Alford told him she was about to start her Christmas shopping and was looking for hints. "What do you want most, Larry?" she asked.

"A new hand, Mom," he answered with a smile. Missy smiled, too, although she knew that her son was being serious. A prosthetic device had been mentioned to Larry from time to time, mainly for various everyday utilitarian purposes, but not for golf. If Larry was to make it as a golfer, he thought, it would be with one hand. Unbeknownst to Larry, Jay Hall had been calling companies that made prosthetic devices to find out whether there was such a thing as an artificial golf hand on the market. At least one company did make such a device, but it was strictly for recreational golfers and did not provide the length and accuracy Larry would need to play competitive golf. Jay also talked with Houston area golf pros, but none of them were aware of anyone having played tournament golf with an artificial hand. Undaunted, he persisted, determined to get a workable prosthesis for Larry.

"We wanted to see to it that Larry had at least a fighting

chance by being able to put two hands on a golf club again,"
said Hall, a good golfer who shoots in the seventies. "But I
found that very little research had been done on sports
prostheses and that there was nothing on the market to
help Larry." So Hall, without any expertise in prosthetics,
decided to design a golf hand for Larry Alford, Jr., on his
own. "First, I had to ask myself just what does the left hand
do on a golf swing for a right-handed player. And the answer
is really quite simple. It holds the club with three fingers
and it hinges or cocks the club. Essentially, it provides those
two functions, and that's about all."

Of paramount importance, Hall knew, was that the hand
had to grip the club firmly enough so that the handle
wouldn't be twisted by the force of the swing. To ensure
that, Hall designed the palm of the hand with pumped-up
air cells. For the wrist, he came up with a ball-and-socket
mechanism which, Hall felt, could perform the function of
a human joint. By the time he was through, Hall had
sketched a hand that, in theory at least, would keep the
club from turning during the swing, provided for a built-in
wrist cock, and ensured that the wrist would not break down
on impact with the ball. "Those are the three biggest
problems golfers have during a golf swing and I think we
had guarded against them."

Swearing Missy Alford to secrecy, Hall took his idea to
Ted Muilenburg, the owner of a prosthetics company in
Houston. "Jay knew nothing about prosthetics and I knew
nothing about golf, but I must say that I was impressed
with his design," Muilenburg said. "The only part of it that
I was worried about was the ball-and-socket joint mechanism.
I wasn't sure it would work, but if it didn't, I figured we'd
find something that would." And Muilenburg did find a
child's knee prosthesis, which he found while rummaging
around in a stockroom at his firm. Lightweight, the
aluminum device would serve perfectly as a wrist for the
golfing hand, Muilenburg was convinced. That wasn't all
that Muilenburg had happened upon. By chance someone
had given him some air cells, which, when inflated, would
fit tightly around the golf grip on the "golfing hand" like
human fingers. Eventually, when he displayed the mold of
the hand he had created, based on Jay Hall's design, both
Hall and Missy, by then his fiancée, looked on in amazement.

"It'll work," Hall said. "I know it's going to work."

Missy, her eyes brimming with tears, tried to envision her son's reaction to the hand. "Just imagine when Larry sees it," she said. But she and Jay decided that he would have to wait about six weeks—until Christmas Day.

Back home, Larry studied under a tutor during a "Homebound" project and played golf almost daily with friends, with his father, and with Jay, shooting in the middle and low eighties. By mid-November he had gained most of his lost weight back and was up to around his normal weight of 160 pounds. *Now if only I can get down into the seventies, maybe I can still make it as the first one-armed golfer on the PGA tour,* he said to himself at one point after a round of eighty. *But it's certainly not going to be easy.* Occasionally, there would be periods of mild depression. At night, Missy often could hear her son tossing and turning, unable to sleep.

"Mom, I really fouled up," he said to Missy one morning after a fitful night's sleep. "I had a chance for a scholarship, and now I've ruined everything,."

Missy looked at him, wishing she could tell him about the hand Jay Hall had designed, if only to cheer him up. "Larry, you're alive and you're all right and that's what matters," she answered. "Everything is going to be fine. And you're still going to go to college."

Missy Alford could hardly wait for Christmas, which was to be celebrated at Jay's house, with his two children from a previous marriage along with Larry and Kristi. There was laughter around the Christmas tree as everyone opened gifts until one gift remained. "Oh, here's one more," Jay said. "It's for Larry."

Unwrapping the box, Larry looked inside, a look of amazement on his face. "It's a hand—my golf hand," he said exultantly.

"It was Jay's idea, Larry," Missy said to her son. "He even designed it."

Overwhelmed with a joyous emotion, Larry threw his arms around Jay. "Thanks, Jay," he said with tears in his eyes. "Thanks very much." For the next few minutes there was not a dry eye in the room amid all the opened Christmas gifts. "Can I try it on, and maybe even hit a couple of balls, Jay?" Larry asked, ecstatic over his surprise gift.

"I'm afraid we can't do that just yet," Jay replied. "Your

arm isn't quite ready for it, and we still have to make some adjustments. Let's wait at least a couple of weeks."

Over the next two months, Jay worked with Ted Muilenburg to adjust and improve the prosthesis. Once the silicone suction sleeve, which slips over the elbow and holds the hand in place, was attached, Larry was able to try it on for the first time. By mid-January, though work still remained to be done, Jay decided to give "The Halford Grip," as he had named it by fusing the names Hall and Alford, a trial run. On the appointed day, Larry could not wait to get to the driving range at The Woodlands Country Club. On the way to the club, Jay tried not to show his own anxiousness.

At the range, wearing his new golfing hand outside for the first time, Larry, starting with a nine-iron, stroked ball after ball right down the middle. "Jay, it feels good, and I can't believe how well I'm hitting the ball," Larry said after hitting a seven-iron as he gradually moved to "longer" clubs. Using his driver, he belted a shot that traveled more than two hundred yards. "Jay, it's great!" Larry said after the tee-shot. "I'm definitely on the way back."

On the way home, Jay Hall felt an inner glow of satisfaction and pride. *Thank God it worked so well the first time out,* he thought. *And after we tune it up and make some adjustments, it's going to be even better.*

In January, Larry returned to McCullough High, where he was greeted warmly by his classmates, some of whom he hadn't seen since before the accident. By March, when Hall and Muilenburg had completed their adjustments on his golfing hand, Larry was on the golf course almost daily, shooting mainly in the low eighties, but occasionally in the seventies. One Sunday he shot a three-over par on the front nine of the north course at The Woodlands. Earlier, in November of 1991, his golf teammates at McCullough organized a fundraiser that brought in $20,000 for Larry's huge medical bills.

Then Johnny Miller, the veteran PGA star and former U.S. Open champion, who had heard about Larry while he was in Houston on business, paid him a visit at The Woodlands. Watching Larry hit balls with his new hand, Miller said, "Larry obviously was a very good player before the accident, and it's obvious to me that he's still very talented. If everything goes well with the prosthesis, I think the sky's the limit as far as his dreams are concerned." Miller, who is active with an amputee organization that teaches people who have lost limbs to play golf, later returned to Houston to take part in a fundraiser.

"Johnny was great, both by getting involved in the fund raiser and by helping me with my game," Larry said. "And we've stayed in touch ever since, both by phone and by letter. I can't thank him enough for the encouragement he gave me."

During his senior year, Larry also returned to the McCullough High team on a limited basis, playing in only a few events and shooting mainly in the mid-eighties, well below what he had done the previous year. "I didn't do as well, but I wasn't surprised because I was still getting used to the new arm." After graduating in May, his game had improved to the point where he felt he was ready to return to the junior tournament circuit, if only on a part-time basis. One of his first tournaments was the Mission Hills Desert Junior tournament in Rancho Mirage, California, where he had tied for second the year before. Competing again against the nation's best junior golfers, Larry did not break eighty during the first two rounds, as he had done in 1991, but on the final day he fired a seventy-seven, a stroke better than during the last round a year earlier. "I didn't finish anywhere near the leaders," he was to recall almost two years later, "but that didn't matter. What mattered most to me was that I had a better final round than the year before, and I did it with my new hand."

Following a semester at a community college in Houston, Larry enrolled at Sam Houston University in Huntsville, Texas, in January of 1993, shortly after Missy Alford and Jay Hall were married. "The people at the University of Houston (which had offered him a scholarship before the accident) talked to me again, and they were nice," he said. "They invited me to try out for the team, but I had to face reality. They have a great college team, and I wanted to play, not sit and watch. And at Sam Houston, where the talent is almost on a par with Houston, I think I can play." Because Sam Houston had a veteran team with a number of outstanding seniors,

Larry "red-shirted" during the spring of 1994, which left him with three years of eligibility starting in 1995. Meanwhile, his golf game continued to improve. In 1993, he twice shot par seventy-two at The Woodlands and, shortly before Christmas of that year, he scored his first hole-in-one on the 157-yard, par-three second hole on his home course.

In the meantime, Jay Hall continued to try to improve on "The Halford Grip." In early March of 1994, Hall obtained an attachment for Larry's golf hand that enabled him to rotate his wrist more effectively. "It's added another twenty yards to my tee-shots and long irons," Larry said, while noting that the rotator enables him to turn the golfing hand over. Larry also developed another interest— speaking to young people in schools and churches, including some who had lost limbs. Outgoing and personable, he related well with youngsters, calling on them not to yield to peer pressures and, in the case of disabled children, telling them that they, too, can overcome their handicaps as he did. "Don't think of your disabilities as something that makes you different—maybe even a lesser person," he said at one church gathering. "Instead, think of your disability as something that can improve your life and make you a stronger person."

Reflecting on his life after the loss of his left hand, young Larry Alford said, "I've learned an awful lot since then. For one thing, I've learned not to take life for granted, and that there's a lot more to my life than just golf, much as I love golf. I no longer get as upset as I used to if I'm not playing well because I realize that it's only a game. And I constantly thank God for saving my life. As time goes on, I realize it's going to become more difficult for me to make it on the PGA tour. But if I don't, that'll be okay because I'll still stay in golf in some way, maybe as a teacher, because I find the game so peaceful. And I want to continue reaching out to young people as a motivational speaker because I sincerely believe I can help them."

In many ways, Larry Alford is the same smiling and friendly young man that he was before his accident. "In a lot of ways, I haven't changed at all," he said with a smile in late winter of 1994. "For instance, my friend, Brendan Donley, and I still go out a lot at night and fish balls out of water hazards at The Woodlands and at some other golf courses. And we still sell them for eighteen cents apiece, just like we did when we were young kids."

CHAPTER 7

DAWN STORRS

Dawn Storrs could not remember a time in her life when she did not love to dance. Perhaps it's because her mother, Barbara, enrolled her in dancing school when she was three years old. She had only been taking lessons for a while when, one day on the way home in the car, she said to her mother, "Mom, I love the dancing. I really do. And when I get big, I want to be a dancer."

Barbara Storrs smiled, delighted that her daughter was enjoying her dancing lessons, but well aware that it could be a passing fancy, as dancing is for many little girls.

But it was not. Dawn's enthusiasm and zest for dancing was coupled with an obvious talent which was manifested early on. By the time she was four, she had given a dance recital at an elementary school in town, displaying poise, stage presence, and talent. As the years went on, her mother and father realized that Dawn was serious about becoming a dancer. From elementary right into high school, she became a familiar figure at talent shows and other school productions in Torrington, Connecticut, as she earned plaudits from audiences for her performances. Meanwhile, she continued to hone her talents at the Doncin School of Dance in Torrington, where she spent several hours of almost every day the year round.

From seventh grade on, Dawn's best friend was Shawn Collins. Though they differed in personality—Shawn was bubbly and more outgoing, while Dawn tended to be quiet and reserved—they became inseparable, sleeping over at each other's houses on weekends, sharing clothes, and later, double-dating. Dawn, a cheerleader in the local Pop Warner football league for kids twelve and under, got Shawn interested and eventually, they both made the cheerleading team at Torrington High School.

If Dawn Storrs in effect taught Shawn Collins how to be a cheerleader, Shawn in turn helped make Dawn more outgoing. Confident, always self-assured, and in complete control before an audience, Dawn was otherwise essentially shy. "Dawn, lighten up and smile," Shawn would sometimes say to her best friend, half-teasingly. "You're too serious." In large measure because of Shawn's encouragement, Dawn began to open up more in high school and become more friendly.

By their junior year at Torrington High, both girls had steady boyfriends and double-dated almost every weekend. In the fall of 1988, Shawn told Dawn that her boyfriend, Tony Mathews, a senior, was taking her to the senior prom in June. "And I already know what I'm going to wear," she said "a lavender gown. It's not my favorite color, but it's the color I want to wear to the prom."

Now it was December, and with the football season over, both Dawn and Shawn, along with the rest of the Torrington High cheerleaders, were now cheering for the boys' varsity basketball team, whose season had just begun. It was December 23 and there was a game that night, the last one before the Christmas vacation. It was also the last day of classes. School was dismissed early, at 1:00 P.M., and Dawn, Shawn, another cheerleader, Beth Masucci, and three boys, all athletes, got into a car and headed for Waterbury to do some last-minute Christmas shopping.

As the car rolled along on Route 8, a mix of snow and sleet began to fall. As it did, Dawn dozed off while her friends chatted and laughed, all aglow with holiday spirit. All of a sudden, the car skidded on the slippery highway and began to career wildly. Sixteen-year-old Beth Masucci screamed while trying to control the car. Her scream awakened Dawn, and soon the car was engulfed in panic. The last thing she remembered was the car hitting a guard rail and her, Shawn Collins, and one of the boys, who were all seated in the back seat, being sucked through the rear window which had blown out on impact.

When Dawn Storrs came to, she found herself lying on a snow-covered grass median divider on the highway. Instantly, she looked down at her legs—her dancing legs, and what she saw shocked her beyond belief. She had landed on a guard rail and her right leg had been practically severed at the knee, hanging together by a thread of muscle tissue. "Oh my God!" she screamed. "My leg! My leg! How will I ever dance again?"

At least Dawn Storrs was alive. About 50 feet away from her lay her best friend, Shawn Collins, who had landed on the highway and been killed instantly. From her vantage point, Dawn could not see Shawn and was unaware of her fate.

Moments after Beth Masucci finally brought the car to a halt, Dawn's boyfriend, David Casale, raced to her side. Casale, though also sitting in the back seat of the car, had been the only one of the four teenagers in the back not catapulted through the window—and only because Dawn had shot up and over him, keeping him from going through also.

Blood gushed from Dawn's right leg. At a glance, Dave Casale saw that the leg had been all but severed. *Stay calm,* he told himself. *Try to do all of the right things now.* Shivering as she lay on her left side, Dawn looked up and said, "Dave, I'm cold and I'm tired. I want to go to sleep. I'm so tired."

Casale quickly took off his leather jacket and sweater, and placed them over Dawn as a number of cars began to stop at the accident scene. "No, Dawn," he said firmly. "You can't go to sleep now. That's the worse thing you can do. So please try—try hard—to stay awake. You've got to stay awake."

As he talked to Dawn, Casale applied pressure to her bleeding right leg with his right hand. Several passersby soon came to their side, and one of them, John Covello, an emergency medical technician, applied bandages to her wound. *God Almighty!* he said to himself. *This kid's leg is hanging by a thread!*

Like Casale, Beth Masucci and a boy who was also sitting in the front escaped serious injury. The third boy in the car, who also had been hurtled through the rear window, lay on the median divider, close by Dawn Storrs, critically injured.

In the emergency room at St. Mary's Hospital in Waterbury, Dr. Patrick Duffy, an orthopedic specialist, and Dr. Barry Pernikoff, a vascular surgeon, closely examined Dawn Storrs' badly mangled right leg. The situation appeared hopeless. Soon the two doctors discussed the possibility of amputation, unaware that Dawn, though lying still, was conscious. "Please don't amputate my leg!" she implored in a weak but clear voice. "If you do, I'll die, because I'm a dancer, and I can't live without dancing."

The two doctors looked at each other, touched deeply by her plea. "We'll try, Dawn," Dr. Duffy said softly. "We'll try." To himself, he thought, *here we have a beautiful sixteen-year-old girl begging us to save her leg, and it's two days before Christmas. We've got to do all that we possibly can to try to save it for her, even though it may take a miracle.*

For almost nine hours, Dr. Duffy, himself the father of five young children, worked on the shattered knee, trying to put it back together. Meanwhile in a nearby room, Dawn's parents and other family members waited and prayed, concerned not for her leg, but for her life, for they had been told about the critical nature of her injuries.

Dr. Duffy quickly found a good sign: the main nerve and vessels were intact. That was extremely important if he were to save the leg. The difficult part now, he realized, was putting all the pieces back together. He knew he would have to use some unconventional means. As the night wore on, he did, fusing parts of the shattered femur bone with wire and then implanting two metal screws to hold the bone in place. But Dr. Duffy had no way of knowing whether it was all going to work. "Anatomically, we had it back together," he was to say in an interview some years later. "But we were still worried about losing the leg to infection, which might make amputation necessary sometime later."

Following the long hours of surgery, Dr. Duffy met with Barbara and Jim Storrs. "The operation is over and we have Dawn's leg back together, at least anatomically," he said softly. "But she's still in critical condition and it's always possible that infection could set in. If it does, we could lose the leg. And I must tell you that even if we do save it, Dawn will never have full use of it again."

It was sobering news to the Storrs. But, they felt, at least Dawn was alive and from what Dr. Duffy said, it sounded like she was going to make it. The leg had become a secondary factor, although both parents held out a fervent inner hope that it could be saved. If she were to pull through but lose her leg, they knew Dawn would be devastated.

"Our main concern is that Dawn lives," Barbara Storrs said.

"Of course," Dr. Duffy replied. "I realize that, and we're doing all that we can to make sure she pulls through."

As Barbara and Jim Storrs prepared to enter the recovery room to see their daughter, Dr. Pernikoff offered a word of caution. "I don't think you should tell Dawn about Shawn," he said. "It's too early for that."

Dawn, though weak and still groggy from the anesthesia, smiled as her parents walked in just before midnight. As they approached her bed, she grabbed her father's hand and asked, "Daddy, do I have my leg?"

"Yes Dawn, you still have your leg," Jim Storrs answered, fighting back tears and unable to tell his daughter that she could still lose it to infection.

Barbara and Jim Storrs braced themselves for the next question, which they knew was coming.

"How about Shawn, Mom and Dad?" Dawn asked. "How is she?"

Trying hard to maintain his composure, Jim Storrs said: "They took Shawn to Waterbury Hospital. We'll keep you posted." Jim Storrs had told the truth. Shawn Collins had indeed been taken to Waterbury Hospital, where the city morgue is located.

By the next morning, Christmas Eve, the Storrs were forced to tell Dawn the truth about her best friend. When they arrived at the hospital, nurses told them that Dawn had been asking constantly about Shawn. "You're going to have to tell her what happened," a head nurse said to them. Reluctantly, the Storrs did, and as they expected, Dawn was devastated. "I would have given both of my legs to have kept Shawn alive," she said, sobbing uncontrollably.

Later that same morning, Dr. Duffy, who had called off a family Christmas vacation trip in order to stay close to Dawn, told her that it would be six months before it would be known if she could keep her right leg. "I also told her that she would probably never be able to dance again, and, most likely would always have to wear a brace," he recalled. "But she looked at me and said, 'Oh yes I will. Just watch.'"

Less than a month after the accident, Dawn received a visit from Tony Mathews, Shawn Collins' boyfriend, a senior at Torrington High. It was an emotional meeting, and eventually, Mathews stunned Dawn when he asked if she could accompany him to the senior prom. Like Dawn, Mathews was convinced that she would not only recover, but that by June she would be able to dance with him at the senior prom. Dawn, of course, was well aware that Mathews had asked her because Shawn was gone and Dawn was her best friend. Tony, having been in Dawn's company so often with Shawn, was very fond of Dawn Storrs as a good friend.

In late January, Dawn finally went home to begin a long rehabilitation. She spent the first month in a wheelchair and then two months on crutches before she was fitted for the first of several braces which she was to wear for two years. She also began therapy sessions to strengthen her leg that lasted for almost two years. Less than a week after returning home, Dawn, accompanied by her parents, went to a basketball game at Torrington High and sat alongside the cheerleaders, her old friends, at courtside. Before the game, she was introduced to the crowd and drew a huge ovation which brought tears to her eyes.

During the next two months, Dawn was also an honored guest at a benefit basketball game at the high school and at a rock concert, both of which were held to raise money to help cover her medical expenses. Together the concert and game raised $5,000. Appearances at both events proved to be deeply moving experiences for the teenager, particularly when she was introduced.

A tutor came to her home daily, and so did many of her friends. That spring, during a visit to Dr. Duffy's office, she told the orthopedic specialist that she was going to the senior prom and not only just to attend, but to dance with her date, Tony Mathews. "He said, 'Okay, because I know you'll go regardless of what I say,'" she recollected, laughing. "But then he said, 'But if you go, you'll have to wear your brace.' And I told him, 'No way. I'm going to the prom, and I'm going without a brace.'"

The night of the prom, as she had vowed to do, she took off her brace. When Tony Mathews arrived to pick her up, he saw Dawn radiant and stunning in a lavender gown, the color that Shawn had told Dawn back in the fall that she would wear to the prom. Dave Casale, Dawn's boyfriend and a longtime friend of Tony's, came by to see her in her prom gown and was there when Mathews arrived. "Remember Tony, you may be taking Dawn to the prom tonight, but don't forget that she's still my girl," Casale said as both Dawn and Tony, along with Dawn's parents, laughed.

At the Farmington Marriott in Farmington, Connecticut, where the prom was held, friends and classmates, many of whom knew Dawn was coming to the prom with Tony Mathews, greeted them warmly. As she had promised she would do, Dawn Storrs danced the night away with Tony— but only to relatively slow dances. "Only slow ones, Tony," she told him when they arrived at the prom. "I don't think I'm quite ready for any of the fast dances yet." As they danced, they chatted and laughed, caught up in the gaiety of the prom, but at times they both fell into silence, thinking of Shawn Collins.

"I'm so glad Tony asked me," she said later. "I know why he asked me to go, and I know my going to the prom with him meant an awful lot to Tony. It was a very special night for both of us."

The following day, her right leg was sore from all of the dancing the night before, and Dawn put on her brace again. She also put in a call to Dr. Duffy. "Dr. Duffy, I went to the prom last night," she said happily. "And I danced, as I said I would, without the brace, and everything worked out fine. Aren't you proud of me?"

Dawn heard Dr. Duffy laugh. "I'd rather you not have taken that brace off, but I knew you would," he said. "But make sure you keep wearing it, and, please, no more dancing until we finish the rehabilitation and therapy."

"I promise," she replied. "And I guess I'll see you soon."

In late August, Dawn began work at a day care center in Torrington. About the same time, she rejoined the Torrington High cheerleading squad as they began preseason drills two nights a week. "But remember," Dr. Duffy told her in advance, "sideline cheers only. And no jumping up and down, and no acrobatics."

In early September, Dawn, still limping slightly, returned to Torrington High for her senior year. That month she also began ballet lessons at the prestigious Nutmen Ballet School in Torrington. It was the one form of dance she had not mastered, and even though she was still wearing a brace, she was determined to do so. First though, she had to tell Dr. Duffy. "I don't think it's a good idea," he said. "If you start dancing at this stage, it can cause problems later on. But I can tell you're going to do it anyway. I tell you one thing and you do another."

Deep down inside, Duffy could not help but admire Dawn's courage and determination. *She's a difficult patient,* he thought to himself. *But she's a great kid. And she's so determined to make it back as a dancer. I only hope that she does, for her sake.*

Dawn began to get discouraged early on during her ballet lessons. Her leg was still weak and her balance was poor, to the point where she fell often. *I can't give up,* she told herself during one particularly difficult session. *I've just got to be patient.* A new flexion knee brace helped, and soon her balance began to improve. Within a few weeks, she was able to catch up to most of the other students.

Dr. Duffy refused to let her shed the brace. Despite the brace, which inhibited her movements, and her limp, Dawn felt by late winter of 1990 that she was prepared to dance again in front of an audience. Taking dance lessons on a fairly regular basis by then, she decided she would perform in the high school's annual "Celebrate the Arts" night on March 24. The setting would be in front of her classmates, parents, school staff members, and others at the Torrington High Little Theatre, where she had appeared so often in the past, thrilling audiences with her jazz and modern dance routines, only now it would be more of a challenge than ever.

The challenge would be far greater, not only because Dawn was still recovering from her critical injury and making her first appearance in front of an audience since the accident, but because she planned to dance routines that she herself had choreographed. Moreover, the dance program would be dedicated to Shawn Collins.

"I'm so nervous—more nervous than I've been before a performance," Dawn told her parents before leaving for the high school the night of the "Celebrate the Arts" program. "I want to show that I can still dance well, and I know I'm going to be thinking of Shawn. I just hope I don't break down."

Like her husband, Barbara Storrs was not at all surprised by Dawn's apprehensive feelings. "Dawn, we know this is a very special night," she said. "But we also know that you're going to do fine. Just try to relax. Everyone knows it's your first time on a stage since the accident. So don't worry."

When Dawn Storrs came on stage that night at the

Torrington High School Little Theatre, the atmosphere was electric. There was not a sound from the capacity audience of about five hundred which included Carol and Larry Collins, the parents of Shawn Collins, along with Barbara and Jim Storrs. First, Dawn and a group of other dancers performed a number of ballet and modern dance sequences to perfection. When they finished, the audience both cheered and applauded.

Then came the dramatic finale—Dawn Storrs alone on stage. With the music of "Let Me Dance for You" from "A Chorus Line" playing in the background, she began a jazz solo. Soon those in the audience—practically all of whom were aware of Dawn's near-crippling injury and how her right leg hung together by a thread of muscle tissue after the accident—were collectively incredulous as she spun about the stage, kicking with *both* legs and leaping in the air. When the dance ended, the response from the audience was deafening—cheers, applause, whistles. Dawn, overwhelmed with joy, bowed again and again, her eyes filled with tears. Then once again, as had been the case several times during her solo, she thought again of Shawn Collins, and suddenly her joy was tinged with sadness. *That was for you, Shawn*, she said to herself, as the applause continued. In the audience, Carol and Larry Collins, tears in their eyes, applauded vigorously, as did Barbara and Jim Storrs. *God, how I wish Shawn had been here to see me*, Dawn thought as she bowed for the last time.

A few days later, Dr. Duffy read about Dawn's performance in a newspaper. He felt a surge of pride in his teenage patient. No way had he ever expected her to be doing such vigorous dancing so soon after her accident, if indeed ever. *I should know by now that whatever Dawn does should not amaze me*, he said to himself. *She's a very special young lady.* He also knew that it would be wrong for Dawn to be overconfident because of her performance. She was still in a rehabilitative process, and it would be a long time, if ever, before she could dance on a regular basis.

Dawn graduated from Torrington High on schedule in June of 1990. That summer she taught dancing at a camp in Torrington and also continued therapy sessions which mainly consisted of lifting weights to strengthen her right leg. Because of the therapy sessions, she decided to put off going to college until the following January. In November, Dr. Duffy removed the two metal screws that he had inserted in her knee almost two years earlier. Her limp became less pronounced and by Christmas time, it was no longer even noticeable.

Before Christmas, Dawn went to New York City to audition for the highly-competitive dance program at The City College of New York in upper Manhattan. During an interview with the director of the Fine Arts program at City College, Carolyn Adams, Dawn told her about the permanent damage she had suffered to her right leg, but that she still wanted to make dancing her career.

Adams had no idea what to expect, but she was impressed by Dawn's determination and resolve. "Why don't you go through some steps for me," she told Dawn. Dawn proceeded to do brief routines in a variety of dances, with no hint of any physical liability. Adams, accustomed to watching some of the country's best young dancers, was highly impressed. "Very, very nice, Dawn," she said. "I certainly couldn't tell there was anything wrong with your leg. If you want to come, we'd like very much to have you in our dance program."

Dawn Storrs had surpassed another hurdle in her comeback.

Before classes began in January, Dawn decided to audition for a national tour the following summer by Dance Olympus, an elite dance company. When she turned up for the audition at the Grand Hyatt Hotel in Manhattan, she found herself competing with about two hundred other young dancers. Only two were picked at the New York tryout—and one was Dawn Storrs! Eventually she became only one of sixteen young dancers selected from about seven hundred aspirants nationwide for a national tour that summer that covered seven major cities over a three-week period. "It was an incredible experience," she recalled. "Not only did I get to dance with some of the country's best dancers, but I got to work under some great dance teachers. And I got to visit cities I had never been to before, like New Orleans, Nashville, St. Louis, and Boston. And my leg held up fine, although it would be sore from time to time."

It would get sore even more often once classes began

at City College. Class days often would include six hours of dancing along with more conventional liberal arts courses. Icing her sore right leg at night became virtually a regular ritual. Despite the soreness, and even occasional pain, she reveled in the routine, particularly the dancing.

Following her freshman year came another coveted dance honor: Dawn was selected to take part in a highly competitive exchange program involving the Harvard University Dance Center and the London Contemporary Dance School. During the exchange program, she spent three weeks at Harvard and three weeks in London performing ballet, jazz, tap, and modern dance routines in front of audiences. Again, the grind of daily dancing resulted in soreness and pain and, at times, swelling in her right knee; but Dawn Storrs was not about to complain. For this was what she had dreamt of doing since she was a little girl, and here she was doing it, not only in America, but in England, too. And she was doing it less than four years after her right leg had all but been severed in a horrifying highway accident that had taken the life of her best friend.

In large measure because of the strain she was putting on her damaged leg, there were occasional setbacks. In September of 1992, at the start of her sophomore year at City College, her right knee collapsed while she was doing a particularly strenuous physical routine at City College. As she held the knee, grimacing with pain, she wondered if Dr. Duffy was right after all—that eventually the dancing would take its toll. *And everything has been going so well,* she thought to herself as other dancer classmates hurried to her side. After she had returned home, Dr. Duffy told Dawn she had torn cartilage in her knee and would need arthroscopic surgery.

"Will I still be able to dance?" she asked him. Dr. Duffy smiled, knowing the question was coming. "Yes, you will," he said. "But even if I said you couldn't, you probably would. But whatever you do, don't start dancing again until I tell you its okay."

For almost three months, Dawn stayed away from dancing. In late November she returned, taking part in a program that she had choreographed with her roommate, Tosha Smart, as a tribute to Shawn Collins. "There was no way I was going to back out," she said. "It was much too special." Did she ask Dr. Duffy whether she could dance again at that stage? "No, I guess I was afraid he might say no," she said.

As time went on and in spite of all the dancing, Dawn Storr's right leg grew stronger. This enabled her to do routines she had been prevented from achieving because of her leg. By her junior year, for example, she was doing a full plié, a knee bend which had been impossible for her to do since returning to dancing after her accident. That in itself was another giant step for the indomitable dancer from Connecticut.

Despite all of her extracurricular work, Dawn maintained a straight-A average and graduated from City College in June of 1994, a full semester ahead of schedule. While in college, she blossomed as a choreographer, which she had begun doing at Torrington High School, displaying a creativity that both impressed and delighted her teachers. She also worked with young dancers in nearby Harlem and performed with the CitiDance Repertory Company, comprised of dancing students at City College.

Though she became a highly-talented dancer in extremely competitive environments, Dawn was well aware that she still had limitations as a performer. In part for that reason, she decided to become a dance teacher and choreographer after her graduation, rather than a professional dancer.

"Becoming a teacher and a choreographer are very realistic goals for Dawn," Carolyn Adams said. "Still, she's an extremely talented dancer and could, in my estimation, become a successful professional dancer. With Dawn, nothing is impossible."

Dr. Patrick Duffy grew increasingly incredulous at his patient's progress and her achievements as a dancer. "What Dawn has done is absolutely unbelievable and a continuous source of amazement to me," he said shortly before her graduation from college in the spring of 1994. "She has done more than we ever possibly thought she could do, especially when you realize we never thought she would ever dance again once we managed to save her leg. And we weren't even sure we could do that.

"I must say that I'm very, very proud of Dawn. It's

been a very emotional experience for me. And she's always stayed in touch, sending me postcards from wherever she goes. She's a remarkable young lady who just wasn't going to give up."

CHAPTER 8

FRANK BICE

If there was one "Big Man on Campus" at Siena College in the fall of 1980, it had to be Frank Bice. Extremely popular among his classmates, the handsome and always-smiling Bice was president of the senior class, captain of the football team and a Small College All-American, and a star lacrosse player. Although he was warm and friendly on campus, he was intensely competitive and aggressive on the playing field. He made up for his small stature—five-feet, ten-inches and 180 pounds—with tenacity and desire. He was also a leader, both in sports and campus life, as he had been since he was in grade school on Long Island. Indeed, at every level, friends and teammates had looked up to Bice.

Early in his senior year at Siena in Loudonville, New York, a suburb of Albany, Bice could hardly be happier. He loved playing football, had tons of friends, and very close ties to his mother who had raised Frank, his two brothers, and three sisters after her husband died when Frank, the youngest child, was two. He was also deeply religious. It was largely because of his religious beliefs that he had attended The Canterbury School, a prep school in New Milford, Connecticut, and Siena, both Roman Catholic institutions.

"Frank was always a natural leader with a special charisma about him," said Terry Regan, Frank's best friend, who had also gone to Canterbury and was Bice's backup at the safety position on the Siena football team. "And he was nice to everyone. For example, he'd go out of his way to talk to a nerdy guy who just about everyone was ignoring. As far as football was concerned, you just tended to play better when Frank was on the field. And when he hit somebody in football, he sacrificed his entire body. It was the only way he knew how to play."

That was particularly evident on October 4, 1980, when Siena met St. John Fisher College of Rochester, New York, in Rochester. Late in the third quarter, Joe Catan, a tight end for St. John Fisher caught a pass and sprinted into the Siena secondary at full speed. Racing up from his safety position, also in full-stride, Bice hit Catan head-on, with Bice's helmet crashing into Catan's right hip. As Bice fell, his vision became unfocused and a ringing sound reverberated in his ears. He knew he had fallen, but he never felt the ground. *Oh my God!* he thought to himself. *I'm paralyzed!* Within moments, teammates and coaches hovered over Bice. "You're going to be all right, Frank," the Siena trainer, a young woman named JoAnn, said to him consolingly. Bice stared at her in silence as he lay on his back with no sense of feeling. *No. I'm not going to be all right,* he said to himself as he looked up at the trainer. *I'm never going to be all right ever again.*

Growing up in Manhassett on Long Island, Bice lived for sports, his family, his friends, and his church. "He played just about every sport, but basketball was his main game," said Gene Miller, a lifelong friend who went on to become an All-American lacrosse player at Boston College. "Frank was always small for his age, but he did not have a complex about it. And he was a fierce competitor in whatever he played. He was a very good point guard in basketball and he did well in other sports, too. Everyone liked Frank. He was a perfect gentleman. But he could get into mischief, and if he did, he would never back down."

The Bice house was always filled with the children's friends, Margaret Bice, Frank's mother, recalls. "Frank, especially, was very gregarious and also very hyper. He had trouble relaxing. I recall how he once got a one hundred percent award—I think it was at Siena—because he was always going all-out. And on Sundays, he was always anxious to go to church. For about four years—from the time he was nine until he was twelve—he was an altar boy. And he loved it. But Frank was no goody-two-shoes. He liked to make people laugh and to have fun."

At The Canterbury School, situated on a beautiful campus in western Connecticut, Bice was an outstanding athlete,

lympic ski team hopeful Ann Walters got to the Olympics faster than her other
nior Development Team members, although by a different route. After breaking
er back in a ski run at 16, she stormed back in multiple wheelchair sports events in
any national competitions and in both the Seoul and Barcelona Paralympics.

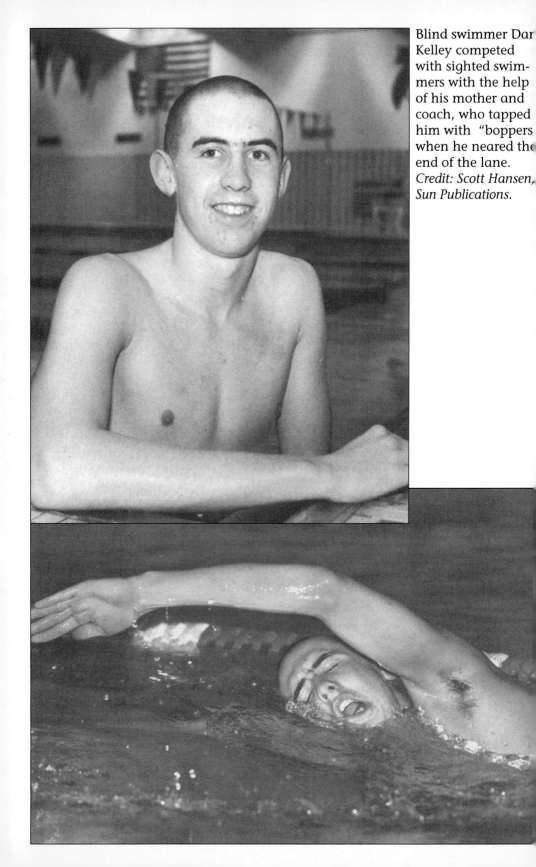

Blind swimmer Dan Kelley competed with sighted swimmers with the help of his mother and coach, who tapped him with "boppers" when he neared the end of the lane.
Credit: Scott Hansen, Sun Publications.

...burgeoning basketball ...r, Chris Samele lost his ... in a car accident, but ...me back with an artificial ... to lead his high school ...m in three-point baskets ...d also star on the tennis ...urt.

Eleven-year-old David Potter batted .429 in Litt[le]
League with an on-base average of .733—and
that's with no arms below the elbow. *Credit: Sto[ck]
Options.*

awn Storrs fought back to compete, perform on-
age, and teach as a dance instructor after her
arly severed right leg was saved by surgeons in
ponse to her pleas.

Dennis Wychocki, who grew up with no arms, never realized he was different than the other kids. His legend as an outstanding placekicker for four years lives on in a tough Chicago high school league, which probably remembers him best for the game-saving body tackle he made on a kickoff return. *Credit: Chicago Tribune.*

he unexpected and
mysterious loss of sight in
her teens did not deter Jeni
Armbruster from playing
competitive volleyball and
basketball. Ultimately, she
played in the Paralympics
for Disabled Athletes in
Barcelona on the U.S.
Goalball Team for blind
athletes.

Sarah Billmeier, who lost her leg to cancer at 5, became one the the world's best disabled skiers, winning three gold medals at the 1992 Paralympics in Albertville, France, at 14, and two golds and a silver in Lillehammer, Norway, in 1994. *Credit: Sharon McNeill.*

natural leader with special charisma, Frank Bice survived a paralyzing neck
jury in a college football game to graduate and become a coach at his prep school
ma mater.

Known as the "One-Armed Wonder," Pete Gray (shown on both pages) was a legend in semi-pro and professional baseball in the 1940s, including one season with the big-league St. Louis Browns in 1945. *Credit: National Baseball Hall of Fame.*

What would seemingly be an insurmountable handicap in broadcasting a baseball game has not been a deterrent to Don Wardlow (left), believed to be the first blind play-by-play broadcaster ever. His partner, Jim Lucas, acts as his eyes.
Credit: Paul Schiraldi.

Most of his victims in the ring did not know that boxer Joe Glen (left) fought, and won, wearing an artificial leg.

The "Dennis Walters Golf Show" was born when PGA prospect Walters, paralyzed in a freak golf cart accident, returned to the game with the aid of a specially designed golf cart and a lot of natural skill.

Larry Alford plays golf with a "golfing" hand, designed by his stepfather after losing his left hand in a car accident when he was a highly ranked junior golfer.

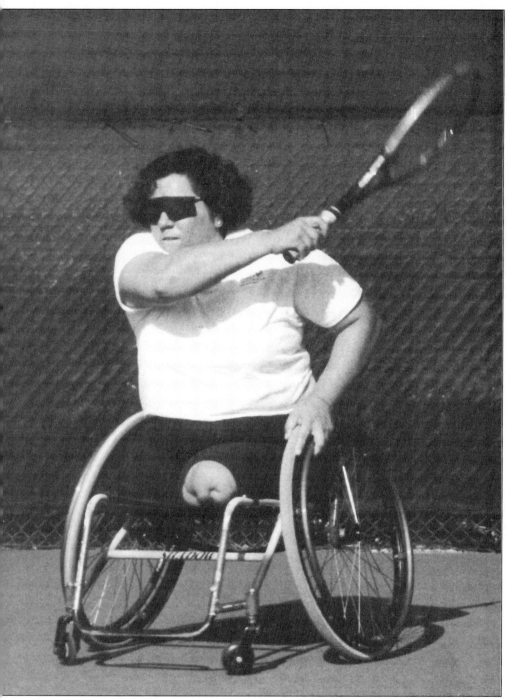

natural athlete before losing her legs in a highway accident, Nancy Olson rose to
. 1 in the nation on the National Foundation for Wheelchair Tennis Grand Prix
cuit.

None of the other Little League baseball teams ever complained about Jonathon Slifka's special arrangement, which included an extra second-baseman in the field and a designated runner when at bat, because Jonathan, born with spina bifida, covered his position in a wheelchair. *Credit: Shana Sureck-Mei, Hartford Courant.*

starring in football, basketball, and lacrosse. Though he missed his friends on Long Island, most of whom stayed home to go to high school, Bice developed many new friendships and fell in love with Canterbury. Very popular among his classmates, Bice emerged as a student leader, and in sports he captained both the football and lacrosse teams in his senior year. "Frank, besides being a terrific athlete, was a terrific kid at Canterbury," recalls Tom Sheehy, who coached him in basketball and is now the headmaster at Canterbury. "He was a tremendous competitor and a leader in every sport he played. And everyone liked him."

The same was true at Siena, which is best known in sports for its Division I basketball team that plays a major college schedule. At Siena, Bice decided to forego basketball and concentrate on football and lacrosse, which by then had become his best sports. "I always loved basketball, but, at five-ten, I doubt if I could have done much at Siena," he said. By his junior year, he had developed into a Small College All-American safety, renown among Siena's opponents for his deadly tackling and reckless style of play. "I was a madman on the football field," he says now with a laugh. "I don't know what got into me when I got out on the field, but looking back, I was a bit wild, I'd say."

Bice does not blame football for his injury. "It was a fluke thing, and it was my fault," he says. "When I went to make the tackle, I put my head down, which you're not supposed to do because of the danger." With Bice out of the game, he was ironically replaced by his backup and best friend, Terry Regan. "It was terrible going out there," recalls Regan, now an advertising executive. "It was impossible to concentrate. All we could think of was Frank."

On the way to Strong Memorial Hospital in Rochester, a priest held Bice's hand and, with Frank, said Hail Mary's one after the other. In the emergency room, x-rays were taken of Bice's neck as he lay on a table, still in his Siena uniform. At one point, Bice said to a doctor, "I broke my neck, didn't I?" The doctor replied, "Yes, you did." Then Frank asked, "Am I going to live?" The doctor responded, "I don't know." Several minutes later, Bice realized that a priest was giving him the last rites of the Catholic church. *Oh my God! This is even worse than I thought,* he said to himself. "Father, I want you to hear confession from me," he said to the priest. *If I'm going to die,* he told himself, *I want to go with a clean slate.*

For about five days Bice hovered between life and death. Terry Regan, and other close friends were permitted to visit with him briefly. The day after the accident, his mother and other members of his family flew to Rochester to be with him. "It's okay, Mom," he said shortly after his mother arrived. "I'm going to beat this. I'm going to walk again." By then though, Margaret Bice had been told by Frank's doctors that he had been permanently paralyzed and would never walk again. The doctors were not even certain that Bice would survive his life-threatening injury. But he did, even though he developed pneumonia and, during his first month in the hospital, lost fifty pounds. Yet, his spirits remained remarkably high, sustained in large measure by all of his visitors, particularly on weekends. "The worse period was Sunday night after everyone had left," he recalls. "That's when I could get real down sometimes."

Several weeks after the accident, Bice was having trouble trying to sleep in the rehabilitation wing of Strong Memorial Hospital. He was in a room with a thirty-year-old paraplegic who had been hospitalized since he was seventeen following an auto accident and was sustained by a special machine that emits the sound of a vacuum cleaner. "Suddenly, the reality sank in—the permanence of it all—that I too, was now a paraplegic," Bice said. "The enormity of it all hit me. But then I was realized that this guy was a lot worse off. I just couldn't imagine having to depend on a machine to stay alive. And I lay there feeling horrible for my new friend."

Later, after being transferred to the famed Rusk Institute in Manhattan, Frank got a surprise visit from his childhood sweetheart, Liz Robb, whom he had not seen since they were in the eighth grade. "Do you remember me, Frank?" she asked after entering the room with two mutual friends. "I'm Liz Robb, your old girlfriend." Bice smiled and tried to extend his right hand. "Of course I do, Liz," he replied with a smile. "How are you?" It is a touching, yet somewhat awkward scene, since they had broken up nine years earlier while they were youngsters, and Liz Robb had since married.

About three months after his accident, Frank was visited by Terry Regan and three other buddies. It was to be only the second time he had left the Rusk Institute—the first time was on New Year's Eve when Regan and some other buddies took him out to celebrate. This time, his pals took him to a New York Islanders hockey game at the Nassau Coliseum on Long Island after telling nurses they will have him back by midnight. But after the game, they convinced Bice to drive to Siena with them, a trip of about three hours. It was already 10:00 P.M. It was to mark Frank's first time back at Siena, and it was to be a very special night. They arrived about 1:00 P.M. at Dapper's, a Siena hangout close by the campus, which is usually deserted late on a Sunday night. But Frank's friends knew he was coming, and the bar was jammed with several hundred students. As Bice entered with his friends, the crowd in the bar erupted with cheers. Bice sat in his wheelchair stunned, incredulous at the turnout. The students surrounded Bice, hugging and kissing him, and the emotional homecoming continued until 4:00 A.M. Three hours later, at 7:00 A.M., Bice was returned to the Rusk Institute by his friends. They apologized for getting him back so late, saying their car had broken down on the way back from Long Island. For Bice, it had been an emotional, but heartwarming and inspiring evening, one that he will not forget.

While at Strong Memorial Hospital in Rochester and at the Rusk Institute, Bice was visited by Joe Catan, the former tight end for St. John Fisher College whom Bice had tackled, resulting in his paralysis. Ill at ease when he was introduced to Bice, Catan told Frank he delayed visiting him because he felt Bice might feel he was to blame for his injury. "It wasn't your fault at all, Joe," Bice told him. "I was responsible for what happened, not you. I put my head down, so it was my fault, not yours." Catan, obviously relieved, shook Bice's hand and said, "I'm glad I finally got to talk to you, Frank. I'm very sorry over what happened, and I want to wish you the best."

Throughout his stay at Rusk, as at Strong Memorial, Bice's frame of mind was good. He became a familiar figure wheeling himself around the Institute, visiting other paraplegics, trying to cheer them up. "Some of these guys felt that their lives were over," a doctor at Rusk recalls. "But Frank, with his smile and good spirits, picked them up and made them feel better about themselves and also more hopeful about the future."

Discharged from the Rusk Institute in June, Bice returned to Siena in late August, both to complete his senior year, which had been interrupted by his tragic accident, and to serve as an assistant football coach. "I vowed never to play again after Frank was hurt," Terry Regan said. "But he called me during the summer and asked me to come back and be his attendant. They had refitted part of the dorm to accommodate Frank, and that made it a lot easier for him. He also talked me into playing again, and as it turned out, I had my best season ever.

"A lot of the guys got choked up during the first couple of two-a-day preseason practices after seeing Frank in his wheelchair on the sidelines," Regan went on. "Emotions ran very high, but Frank was very inspiring and things worked out fine. The most emotional day of all, I guess, was when we played St. John Fisher (at whose field in Rochester Bice had been paralyzed the previous fall). Before the kickoff, players from both teams gathered at midfield, kneeled down and said a prayer for Frank." Deeply moved, Bice on the sideline in his wheelchair, looked out at the players intently with a warm smile. When the game ended, the entire squad from St. John Fisher made a beeline for Frank, surrounding him, shaking his hand and wishing him well. Several embraced Bice, who was deeply touched by the mass outpouring of affection.

It was a fall marked by many emotional experiences for Frank Bice. One of the most dramatic moments occurred when Terry Regan and some of his closest friends presented him with a check for $50,000 to help cover his astronomical medical expenses. The money had been contributed by Siena students and faculty, alumni, and area businessmen, many of whom had been fans of Bice's when he starred on the gridiron. Again, he was deeply moved by the heartwarming gesture.

After graduating from Siena in June of 1981, Bice was uncertain about his future. Returning home to Manhasset to live with his mother, he took a job as a public relations representative with the New York Telephone Company. Evenings and weekends, he coached junior league teams in basketball, and both boys and men in lacrosse. "I loved the coaching, and I knew that I was being called to some kind of service—to a 'calling,'" he recalled. "Finally, I talked to a priest I knew and decided to enter a Roman Catholic seminary in Huntington." That was highly unusual, since it is extremely rare for a paraplegic to be accepted as a prospective priest. "I guess they knew that Frank Bice is a very, very special type of person," another lifelong friend, Jay Ryan, now a financier, said.

Before Bice entered the seminary, he was an assistant to Walter France, the coach of the eighth-grade boys basketball team at St. Mary's Parochial School in Manhassett, the school he attended before going to Canterbury. "We had about fourteen kids on the team, and at first about half of them would ride with me and the rest with Frank in his specially-equipped van (which friends and other townspeople in Manhassett bought for Bice for $35,000)," said France, who had coached Bice at St. Mary's. "But before long, all fourteen of them would hop into Frank's van, and I would drive to the game by myself. That's how much they liked Frank. And when we got to a gym, a couple of the kids would pick up Frank, wheelchair and all, and carry him up and down the stairs and into and out of the van. They were crazy about him."

That season, during the playoffs, France was unable to come to the first game and asked Bice to take over. Bice was understandably nervous since St. Mary's was playing St. Aidens School on their court in Williston Park on Long Island. In two regular season games, as Bice recalled, "they killed us," and St. Aidens was heavily favored in the playoff game. On a hunch, Bice started Tom Blake, a seldom-used player who proceeded to play the game of his life as St. Mary's upset St. Aidens. Ten years later, Bice and Blake met at a mall at Christmas time in Hicksville on Long Island. "One of the first things Tom said to me was that he still hadn't forgotten, nor will he ever, how I started him in the playoff game, and how it meant so much to him," Bice said. Recalls Blake: "Frank had a lot of faith in me, and I never played better. He was something special as a coach. He was so motivated, and he gave you such a lift as a player and a person. He certainly had a tremendous impact on me."

During his first three years at the seminary, Bice was completely away from coaching. But in his fourth year—his "pastoral year"—he spent the time teaching at St. John the Baptist School in West Islip. Early on he became aware that the school needed a junior varsity football coach and volunteered for the job. At the first practice session, he was extremely apprehensive. "I was scared stiff," he recalled. "I remember how one kid approached me and said, 'You're our coach?' And I said, 'Yes, I am.' And the kid, looking at me incredulously, says, 'Are you sure?' I laughed and assured him that I was." Before long, Bice established a good rapport with the players, who were soon to forget that he was in a wheelchair. Later, while at St. John the Baptist, he became a popular coach of the junior varsity basketball and lacrosse teams. The more he coached, the more he realized how much he loved doing it, and how much he enjoyed teaching and working with young athletes. Only a year away from being ordained as a priest, Bice began to have doubts whether the priesthood was indeed his calling.

Those doubts intensified in the spring of 1990 after he encountered his previously mentioned childhood sweetheart, Liz Robb, in a Long Island restaurant while they were both out with friends. They chatted for a while and Bice learned that Liz, who has two daughters, had just gone through a divorce. They exchanged phone numbers, and a week later, he phoned his old sweetheart and they went out "for some laughs." Before long, Bice recalls, "I realized I'm falling in love with Liz. But here I am in a seminary, a year away from becoming a priest, and I'm in a wheelchair." Finally, in December of 1990, Bice decided to leave the seminary, both because of his love for Liz Robb and his yearning to get back to coaching kids. "My experience in the seminary was great," Bice says. "Everyone was wonderful to me. I got to visit the Vatican twice and met the Pope on both occasions. And he remembered me the second time! What an experience! But I felt that I wanted to have a family and became more and more convinced that coaching, and not the priesthood, was really my calling."

After leaving the seminary, Bice phoned his old coach, Tom Sheehy, the headmaster at The Canterbury School. Fortuitously, there was an opening on the staff—to teach theology and Spanish. Bice jumped at the opportunity to return to his alma mater in the fall of 1991. Then when Sheehy asked if he were interested in coaching the junior varsity football team, Bice, ecstatic at the chance, told him he was sure he could get the job done. "In prep school, I remember Frank as a rambunctious kid with a tremendous amount of drive who worked hard to make himself a great student and athlete," Sheehy said. "He was always a leader, and at Canterbury he's become a great role model for the kids. They see him in his wheelchair, smiling and enthusiastic and loving what he's doing, and they go all out for him."

By his second year at Canterbury, Bice was head coach of the football team, and the coach of the junior varsity basketball and lacrosse teams. During Bice's early days as a teacher and coach at Canterbury, the school's sports teams fell on hard times. His first varsity football team failed to win a game, and that winter the varsity basketball team endured a horrendous season. Midway through the season, the Canterbury Cagers had not won a game. Two players quit in frustration and three others were on the verge of quitting. Word of the defections got to Bice, who in turn asked Sheehy if he could address a student assembly in late January of 1993. To a spellbound student body, Bice, in his wheelchair on the stage, told a story about Vin Carafora, a former teacher and coach he had met at the Rusk Institute. Bice recounted how, at the age of twenty-six, Carafora became a quadriplegic after an insect bite that virtually destroyed his nervous system. Although bedridden for years and barely able to get around in his wheelchair, Carafora and his wife eventually adopted six children ranging in age from six to eighteen.

"He can't teach and he can't coach. He can hardly do anything," Bice tells the hushed assembly. "But he is full of life and full of love, and he never quits, even though his dreams have been dashed."

The next day the captain of the Canterbury varsity basketball team, one of those who had quit the squad, went to Bice and said, "Mr. Bice, I made a big mistake and I want a second chance. I want to rejoin the team. Can you please tell the coach?" Bice did, and the captain and the other player who had quit, along with the three who were prepared to leave, rejoined the varsity. There was no doubt that Bice's dramatic talk the day before had made them change their minds about quitting.

Bice himself suffered a personal setback that spring when he and Liz Robb broke off their engagement, at least temporarily. Ironically, logistics turned out to be a key element in the breakup. Under her divorce decree, Liz Robb, who works on Wall Street, could not take her children more than fifty miles from New York City, where her since remarried ex-husband lives. Canterbury, in New Milford, Connecticut, is more than eighty-five miles away. "I still love Liz, and I hope we can work something out," Bice said in the summer of 1982 while working as a counselor at the Shake-A-Leg Camp at the University of Rhode Island in Kingston. "And I'm crazy about her two girls."

Rarely does Bice talk about the accident that resulted in his paralysis. But he did allude to it during a football game in October of 1992, his first year as head coach. Bice, impeccably attired as always in a blue blazer, dress shirt and tie, could tell that his players were in a down mood. They had lost all five of their games to date and now, in their sixth game against Westminister of West Hartford, they were losing, 39–7—and it was only halftime. In the locker room, Bice sensed the collective despair. Until now, no matter how badly Canterbury was losing, Bice would exude optimism. "We can beat these guys, I know we can," he would say, exhortingly, while knowing deep down that Canterbury had no chance of winning. But on this Saturday afternoon, again playing a far superior Westminister team, Frank Bice decided to take a new tack.

"I know we're going to lose this football game," Bice said to his charges, most of whom sat with their heads down. Stunned at Bice's words, the Canterbury players looked up in unison at their coach, incredulous that he was conceding defeat. "Twelve years ago on a football field, I also lost," Bice went on to his small but enrapt audience. "But every day since then I've put on my helmet, so to speak, and gone out to play, knowing that I'm still going to lose. But I keep playing the game. And now I want you all to put on your helmets and go out and play the rest of the game as hard as you can even though you're going to lose."

This was no Knute Rockne "Win one for The Gipper" halftime oration, intended to inspire his players to great heights and victory over a superior foe. Rather, it was Frank Bice's way of telling his young players not to quit, no matter how great the adversity, whether it be in sports or in real life. On this Saturday afternoon in New Milford, Connecticut, on the beautiful Canterbury campus, Bice's message took hold. Inspired and fired up by their coach's halftime talk, the Canterbury players came back to outplay and outscore Westminister in the second half, even though they fell short of victory. "It was the best half we played all season," Bice said. "And the kids were still sky-high after the game. Apparently my message got through."

A message, no doubt, that those Canterbury football players will carry with them for the rest of their lives—a legacy from their courageous and inspirational coach.

CHAPTER 9

PETE GRAY

Racing in at breakneck speed, the St. Louis Browns' left fielder made a dazzling knee-high catch of a sinking line drive by New York Yankee outfielder Bud Methany to end a Yankee scoring threat in the third inning. It would have been an outstanding catch if Gray had made it with two hands, but Pete Gray did not make two-handed catches. As was the case with every ball hit his way, Gray caught Methany's liner with one hand, his left hand—the only one he had.

The catch was one of a number of sparkling fielding plays that Gray made on Sunday, May 20, 1945, during a doubleheader between the Browns (who later became the Baltimore Orioles) and the Yankees at old Sportsman's Park in St. Louis, which the Browns shared with the Cardinals. As he often did in all eight pre-expansion American League cities during the 1945 season, Gray electrified the St. Louis crowd with his exploits, clearly demonstrating that in spite of his handicap, he was capable of doing something no one had thought possible—play the outfield in the major leagues, and play it well, with only one arm.

True, 1945 was a war year and playing rosters had been decimated by the military draft and enlistments in the armed forces. But Gray made it to the big leagues on merit, mainly on the basis of an outstanding season with the Memphis Chicks of the Double-A Southern Association in 1944. That year, Gray batted .333, hit five home runs, stole sixty-eight bases to tie a league record, led the league's outfielders in fielding, and was named the Southern Association's Most Valuable Player.

When the Browns, after winning their first and only

pennant in 1944, bought Gray for a reported $20,000 that fall, he said, "I can play with those fellows up there, and I'd like the chance to show them." And show them he did. Everywhere the Browns played during the 1945 season, fans flocked to see the "One-armed Wonder," as Gray was called in the press. From the start, Gray's manager, Luke Sewell, a former big league catcher, told him, "Don't expect any favors," Gray once recalled. "And I told him, 'I don't want any.'"

Gray got off to a good start as Sewell platooned him in left and centerfield against right-handed pitchers. Early in the season, pitchers tried to overpower the skinny six-foot tall, 150-pound Gray with inside fast balls on the theory that he would not be able to get his heavy thirty-eight-ounce bat (far heavier than that used by most big-leaguers) around quick enough with one arm. But Gray, grasping the bat near the end and holding it about a foot in back of him, thrived on such pitches, perhaps he once noted, because he had had to contend with so many of them over the years. At any rate, he would pull such pitches, often on line drives to right field, for base hits. "It wasn't until pitchers changed their tactics and began giving him slow, breaking stuff that Pete began to have trouble," said Don Gutteridge, who played second base for the 1945 Browns.

As a little boy, Petey Wyshner (who later took the name of Pete Gray) loved sports, particularly baseball, which he played with a passion on cold dust-covered fields and sandlots in his hometown of Nanticoke, Pennsylvania, in the heart of a major coal-mining region. By the time he was five, little Pete, who was born right handed, was already showing promise as a ballplayer, especially as a hitter. But when Petey was six, as he and some of his friends were inclined to do, he jumped onto a farmer's wagon and fell off. As he did, his right arm became entangled in a wheel spoke of the horse-drawn wagon. "The farmer put me on his wagon and drove me home, leaving me on the front porch because nobody was home," Gray recalled during an interview in Nanticoke in the late 1980s. "It hurt something awful, and a lady who was a neighbor saw me crying. When she saw what had happened, she called a doctor, and they took me to the hospital and cut off my right arm above the elbow."

Little Petey Wyshner was devastated by the loss of his arm and for years he merely watched his friends play ball.

"After the accident, I was just the batboy," he said. "The other kids figured I couldn't play anymore, and I guess I thought that too, even though I wanted to try. Then one day, when I was about twelve, they needed a player and they let me play. I guess I did okay, because after that they let me play every day. At first I would catch the ball, put the ball and glove on the ground, and then pick up the ball and throw it.

"Then one day an engineer on a coal train was watching me shag fly balls and he said to me, 'Kid, you're pretty good, but you have to learn how to get rid of the ball faster.' After that, I started trying different ways until I came up with the idea of putting the glove under the arm pit after I caught the ball, and letting the ball roll across my chest and then catching it and throwing it. I also found it easier to catch the ball if I took the padding out and let my pinkie stick out. As far as hitting was concerned, it was hard at first, but then I got better and better, maybe because I worked so hard at it. One thing I would do was take a broom handle and some rocks to practice my hitting. I'd tuck the broom handle under my stump, flip the rocks in the air, and then hit them with the broom handle. After a while, I'd hardly ever miss, and I could hit those rocks a mile.

"After a while, like a lot of my friends, I dreamed of playing in the big leagues, preferably with the Yankees, who were always my favorite team. But the older I got, I began to tell myself it was out of the question. After all, whoever heard of a one-armed ballplayer? But I loved the game, and I guess I practiced longer and harder than most kids. I also kept telling myself, 'Pete, the whole thing is confidence in yourself. If you're sure you can do it, you'll do it.'" Before long, not only was Petey Wyshner as good as his friends, he was better. "When I was in my teens, we had a team in Nanticoke called the 'Litz,' for Lithuanians (which Gray was) and I led the team in hitting. About that time, a black semipro team came to Nanticoke to play that had a one-armed outfielder. But he struck out every time he got up, and I knew then that I was better than he was, and he was a lot older than me."

Word of Gray's prowess, particularly as a hitter, began to spread in the Scranton area (Scranton is about thirty-five miles from Nanticoke), and by the time he was sixteen he was earning about $100 a week playing for semipro teams in Scranton and Wilkes-Barre. Gray did so well that when he was seventeen, he went to a St. Louis Cardinal tryout camp in nearby Minersville. "The scout running the tryout asked me my name, and I told him it was Pete Gray. My older brother, Whitey, was fighting as a middleweight under the name of Gray, and so I decided to use it too. But it didn't do me any good at the tryout camp, even though I thought I did pretty good. After that, I hitchhiked all the way to Hot Springs, Arkansas, to a baseball camp being run by a guy named Ran Doanes. When he saw I had only one arm, he looked at me like I was nuts, but he decided to give me a chance after I told him I hitched all the way from Pennsylvania. Then he had this guy named Johnny Mostil, who had played with the Chicago White Sox, hit about a hundred fly balls to me, mostly to my right side, figuring I probably couldn't get to them. But I caught everything and Doanes just rubbed his eyes like he couldn't believe what he was seeing. Then he told me, 'Kid, you can stay here all summer if you want, but in the meantime I'm gonna call some clubs.' And he did. He called a bunch of D league teams and raved about me. But when he told them I only had one arm, they would tell him to forget about it and hang up on him. Finally, I got discouraged and went home, even though Doanes said I could stick around and he'd pay all my bills."

Over the next few years, Gray went to Florida on his own hoping to get a tryout with big league teams, but the trips proved to be fruitless. "Nobody would even give me a shot," he said. "Their attitude seemed to be, 'Whoever heard of a one-armed ballplayer?'" Meantime, Gray continued to star with semipro teams in the Scranton area, consistently batting over .300, fielding brilliantly, and flashing his blazing speed, both on his patented drag bunts and on the bases. All the while he never gave up hope of making it to the major leagues.

Finally, in 1939, when Gray was twenty-four, he got an opportunity that was to lead him into the minor leagues and ultimately, to the majors. In New York with some friends for the 1939-40 World's Fair, Gray, carrying his glove and baseball spikes, rode the subway to Dexter Park in Brooklyn. It was the home of the Bushwicks, a leading semipro club in the 1930s, 40s, and 50s, which was an amalgam of former major and minor leaguers and promising young players. There was a game that night and Gray, waiting outside, asked an employee of the club to point out Max Rosner, the team's owner, when he arrived. The employee did and Gray, with considerable trepidation, approached Rosner, introduced himself, and asked for a tryout.

Though he had a flair for showmanship and gimmickry, Rosner was skeptical and tried to brush Gray aside. But Gray persisted, pulling out a ten-dollar bill and saying, "Look, here's ten bucks. Take it, and if I can't play, then keep the money." Rosner, impressed with Gray's spunk and persistence, smiled and said, "Put the ten dollars away and come on inside. We'll see what you can do." Taking batting and fielding practice before the Bushwicks' game that night, Gray fascinated Rosner, who quickly became aware of not only his remarkable baseball skills, but his potential as a drawing card. Rosner signed Gray to a contract that night, and he was not to be disappointed. In fourteen games with the Bushwicks and the Bay Parkways, another Brooklyn semipro club owned by Rosner's brother, Jack, Gray hit .449 and played errorless ball.

The following year, Jim Skelton, another semipro player from the Scranton area, recommended Gray to the management of the Three Rivers, Quebec club in the "outlaw" Canadian-American League, with which Skelton had played. "Unfortunately, Jim didn't tell them that I only had one arm, so when I got there, they thought I was an impostor," Gray said. "But they figured since I had made the trip and was there, they might as well give me a tryout. I guess I did okay because they put me in uniform that night.

The news that they had signed a one-armed guy got around and there was a big crowd, but the manager kept me on the bench even though the crowd was chanting, 'We want Gray!' Finally, in the ninth inning, he calls on me to pinch-hit. It was just like in the movies. We were losing 1-0, and the bases were loaded with two out in the last half of the ninth. I remember that the count went to two-and-one, and then I lined a pitch to right that scored two runs and won the game. The next thing I knew, everybody was throwing money at me as I ran off the field. I stopped to pick most of it up, and later I counted about $500."

Gray finished the season as the club's most popular player, batting a very creditable .328. After spending the next season playing semipro ball in Scranton and Wilkes-Barre, Gray returned to Three Rivers, which by then was a Class C club in organized baseball, and hit .381. One of his hits was a 417-foot home run, with one arm!

Baseball people throughout the country began to notice Gray. By now it was evident that he was no sideshow attraction but a legitimate ballplayer. In 1943 Gray wound up at Toronto, then in the Triple-A International League. Early in the season, Gray, always outspoken, made the egregious mistake of criticizing manager Burleigh Grimes, who had managed the Brooklyn Dodgers in 1937-38, during a hotel lobby bull session within earshot of Grimes. The next day Grimes released Gray. In doing so, he did him a favor, since Gray was soon signed by the Double-A Memphis Chicks.

Gray proceeded to hit .305 with Memphis and became the biggest gate attraction in the history of the American Association. Then came his remarkable MVP year in 1944, which prompted Browns' owner Donald Barnes to bring him to St. Louis. That fall, Gray was voted "the most courageous athlete of the year" by Philadelphia sportswriters. His remarkable exploits as a player began to serve as an inspiration to servicemen who had lost limbs during World War II, which was still raging in Europe and the Pacific. Wire services circulated a photo of Gray in his Browns' uniform autographing a baseball for a G.I. who had lost an arm in battle.

Even though the Browns had practically the same team that had won the 1944 American League pennant, Gray, as a thirty-year-old rookie, played in seventy-seven games, half of the club's schedule. Particularly during the Browns' first swing through the league, he was a huge gate attraction. Despite the war, the Browns had some solid players, such as first-baseman George McQuinn, Gutteridge, shortstop Vern Stephens, outfielders Mike Kreevich and Gene Moore, and pitchers Nelson Potter, Bob Muncrief, and Al Hollingsworth. By today's standards he did not do badly; indeed players nowadays make millions for having seasons nowhere near as good as Gray's. Appearing in seventy-seven games, Gray had fifty-one hits—forty-three singles, six doubles and two triples—in 234 times at bat for an average of .218, while striking out only eleven times and drawing thirteen walks. Had the Browns been a weak club, Gray probably would have played more, if only for his gate appeal. But the Browns were a contender, involved in a pennant race through most of the season (they eventually finished third), with a plethora of good outfielders who had helped them win the pennant the year before. Even at that, Gray was resented by a number of his teammates who felt he was being used more as a gate attraction than for the good of the team. Kreevich, for one, a .301 hitter the previous year, did not take kindly to sitting on the bench while Gray played what had been Kreevich's centerfield position. The exasperated Kreevich finally quit the team in August and was waived to the Washington Senators.

Years later, Luke Sewell, Gray's manager at St. Louis, hinted that he had been pressured by the club's front office to play Gray late in the season when he had slacked off in his hitting. "I think he was being exploited as a gate attraction," Sewell said. Still, Sewell conceded that Gray could play. "He got off to a good start, and he was okay, particularly the first time around the league. His wrist was strong and he could jump on the fast ball, even against Feller (Bob Feller, the great Cleveland Indians' pitcher, who returned in 1945 after serving almost four years in the Navy). But when they started throwing him junk, he would be way in front of the ball. And the infielders started to play in to take away from the drag bunt, which he was very good at."

Still, Gray had some memorable games, such as during the previously mentioned doubleheader against the Yankees in St. Louis on May 20, 1945. On that day, the "One-Armed Wonder" did it all. Leading off in the first inning against Atley Donald, a veteran mainstay of the Yankee pitching staff, Gray lashed a single to center and then scored the first of what was to be a seven-run inning for the Browns. Coming up for the second time in the inning, Gray lined another fast ball to right, driving in a run, and chasing Donald from the mound. Two innings later, batting against Bill Zuber, Gray stroked his third straight hit, a solid single to center that knocked in another run.

Gray failed to hit safely in his next two times at bat, but by then the Browns were far out in front and the pressure was off. In the field, using his shorn-of-stuffing glove, which is now on display at the Baseball Hall of Fame in

Cooperstown, New York, Gray handled three fly balls flawlessly as the Browns romped to a 10-1 victory. In the second game, Gray slacked off somewhat, going one-for-three, but in the field he put on a spectacular display. In the first inning he leaped against the left field fence to take away an extra-base hit from Yankee shortstop Frank Croseeti. Then in the third inning, he made his glittering catch of Bud Methany's liner. Later, Gray, who had remarkable balance despite his disability, sprinted to the bleacher wall in left center to snare drives by Johnny Lindell and Oscar Grimes—balls that probably made seven putouts in the second game—scooped up a half-dozen base hits, and after a quick bit of fielding legerdemain with glove and ball, rifled the ball in to keep runners from advancing. For Gray, and the 20,507 fans at Sportsman's Park, it was a day to remember. "All in all," wrote *New York Times* sportswriter James Dawson in his account of the doubleheader, "the one-armed Pete Gray was a positive menace."

Watching Gray play the outfield was as fascinating as observing him at bat. After catching a fly ball, Gray, using one swift, fluid motion, would bring his glove up to his right arm pit, letting the ball roll down his wrist and across his chest. With his glove tucked under his right stump, he would then drop his left hand in time to catch the ball and then throw it in. On ground balls, Gray would scoop up the ball in his glove, toss the ball in the air, drop his glove to the ground, catch the ball and then fire it in to a base, to home plate or to a cutoff man. Although he had been born right handed, Gray had developed a strong left arm, and base runners soon learned not to take liberties with it. None of the Yankees tried to take an extra base on him during the doubleheader, but three American Leaguers who did during the 1956 season were thrown out.

Gray's dour personality proved to be a liability. Don Gutteridge and a number of Gray's former Browns' teammates portrayed him as a surly, complex individual with a deeply-rooted inferiority complex, who became enraged whenever anyone showed any signs of pity or sympathy towards him. "Pete always thought people were feeling sorry for him, even when they weren't," said Gutteridge who went on to manage the Chicago White Sox and was a scout for the Los Angeles Dodgers until he retired at the end of the 1992 season. "He always seemed to have a chip on his shoulder and would resent it if you tried to help him in any way. He was very self-sufficient, and there wasn't anything he couldn't do by himself. But I certainly marveled at him. He could do things in the outfield that some of our other outfielders could not."

Another former teammate, Ellis Clary, the Browns third-baseman in 1945, said, "Pete was the most ornery S.O.B. I ever met. You'd feel sorry for him and want to help him the first day you met him, and by the next day you'd hate his guts. I think he was basically a good guy, but he had this terrible complex about the missing arm. But he could certainly play ball. He was no sideshow, but a good ballplayer. If he'd only had a better attitude, he might have stayed up. I think he also made the other outfielders hustle more because they resented sitting on the bench while a one-armed guy was playing, said Clary who went on to scout for the Minnesota Twins and the Toronto Blue Jays.

Because of his argumentative nature and super-sensitivity, Gray never did endear himself to his teammates. On several occasions, he got into heated arguments with members of the club. "He took swings at a couple of guys, but they just backed off and wouldn't swing back," Clary said. One player who did swing back was Sig Jakucki, a massive, roistering, heavy-drinking pitcher who, at least on the surface, showed absolutely no compassion towards Gray. "We were waiting for a train in Toledo after an exhibition game and someone took a few fish out of a barrel on the train platform and, unknown to Pete, put them in his left pocket where he kept his cigarettes," Clary recalled. "When Pete reached for his cigarettes and found the fish, he immediately suspected Jakucki and went at him, punching him in the stomach. Jakucki, who outweighed Pete by about ninety pounds, said, 'Okay, I'll fight you, you S.O.B., but to make it fair, I'll keep one hand behind my back.' They both landed a couple of punches before some of the guys broke it up. Jakucki was so big and powerful he could have killed Pete, even with one hand. And I think a lot of the guys were rooting for him."

For Gray, the highlight of his only big league season was playing in Yankee Stadium. Busloads of fans from Nanticoke and the Scranton area came to New York whenever the Browns came to the "House that Ruth Built."

"The first time we played in New York was the only time my folks got to see me play in the big leagues," Gray recollected. Despite rain, 38,378 fans turned out at Yankee Stadium on Sunday, May 27, many drawn to see "The One-Armed Wonder," who went one-for-three. During a subsequent trip to New York, Gray went three-for-five against his once-favorite team, the Yankees. But Gray's fans, and they were legion, were disappointed during the last game he ever played at Yankee Stadium, on September 19, when after being thrown out on a close play at first base in the first inning, he was kicked out of the game for protesting a call by umpire Bill McGowan. That was in keeping with Gray's nature, since he argued with umpires about as much as he did with his teammates.

Gray's 1945 season with the Browns was the last wartime year. In 1946, with the Browns' roster crowded with returning war veterans, he was sent to Toledo to the Triple-A American Association, where he batted a respectable .285. Then, after seasons with Elmira in the Eastern League and Dallas in the Texas League, Gray dropped out of organized baseball and barnstormed for a year with the House of Davis, a peripatetic collection of semipros whose beards were the team's trademark. "After my one season with the Browns, they arranged a barnstorming trip for me in California," Gray said. "We played about eight games against the Pacific Coast League all-stars, and I got $1,000 a game. So I made more in two weeks than the $5,000 I did for the whole season with the Browns." Gray could have made a lot more. Hollywood offered him $25,000 to make a movie about his life. He refused after learning that Monte Stratton, a big league pitcher who had lost a leg in a hunting accident in the 1930s, had earned more than three times as much to let Jimmy Stewart portray him in the film, "The Monte Stratton Story." Years later, in the 1980s, Gray finally relented and permitted a television movie to be made about him, starring Keith Carradine.

From the time he left baseball, Gray's source of income remained a mystery. "I've never worked a day in my life outside of baseball," he told this writer during an interview in Nanticoke in the mid-1980s. How did he survive? "Well, I was always pretty good at poker, dice, and pool," he said with a smile, seated at a table in the Town Tavern, a popular local hangout owned by a cousin, Bertha Vedor. He visited the tavern every morning, though he was forced to stop his heavy drinking in the late 1970s following major stomach surgery. For years, Gray was known as one of the best pool-shooters in the Scranton area, not disinclined to do a little hustling from time to time. Right into his seventies, he was also an avid golfer, playing the game almost every day, always for some side bets. As a golfer, Gray was almost as remarkable as he was a baseball player, shooting in the low eighties, and at times the high seventies, and driving most of his tee-shots more than 200 yards down the middle. A man of extremely modest means—he never had a phone, for example, while living alone in the twelve-room house where he grew up and where he stayed after his parents, two sisters, and brother had died—he refused to appear at baseball card shows, a source of revenue for many former players. Nor would he ever accept invitations to attend oldtimers' games. "I don't want to go anywhere, except a ball game at Yankee Stadium once or twice a year," he said during the summer of 1993. "I just want to stay in Nanticoke and be left alone."

And he was left alone, refusing practically every attempt at an interview, and rarely leaving the Hanover section of Nanticoke where time seemed to have stood still for decades. Like clockwork, he would drop in to the Town Tavern every day to talk to old friends, either wearing an overcoat or with an overcoat or jacket draped over his right stump. Then he would stroll down Front Street—Gray never drove a car—stopping to talk to more old friends and dropping in on storekeepers. To a visitor it is surprising to note the absence of any lasting tribute to Gray, far and away Nanticoke's biggest all-time celebrity. No baseball fields, nor anything else for that matter, are named for perhaps the most unusual baseball player of all time. Apparently no one in Nanticoke ever gave the idea any thought. But it never bothered Gray, or at least so he said. "I don't want anything named after me," he once said. "And if they tried to do it, I wouldn't let them." Since leaving the game as a player in the early 1950s, Gray's only connection with baseball involved his attendance at Little League games and other sports events in Nanticoke. For years, youngsters in the town were incredulous when told that Gray had played in the major leagues. "They'd ask me how I could throw the ball after I caught it, and how I could hit. And sometimes I would show them," he said.

For most of the time after he left baseball, Gray was largely a forgotten man in spite of his extraordinary accomplishments. But then, starting in the late 1980s, many people of whom had never heard of Gray before, began to try to get in touch with him. "It was because of the movie and the Jim Abbott thing, I guess," he told me in the summer of 1993. Gray was referring to the belated movie about his life and to Abbott, the pitcher who made it to the big leagues though he was born without a right hand.

Gray, always somewhat cantankerous, hardly seemed delighted at being remembered. "I'm getting so much stuff that I'm sick of it," he told me. "Some people send me whole boxes of balls to sign, along with a little money. But I think they sell the balls and make money off me." As for Abbott, Gray was not entirely surprised at his success. "I've always felt that if another one-armed or one-handed guy was going to make it, it would be as a pitcher. But you're never going to see a one-armed fielder again. Sometimes I wonder how I did it." Despite his protestations about the mail, his cousin, Bertha Vedor, said, "I think he likes getting it." Nanticoke mailman Chet Pientka agreed. "I think he used to throw it all away. But then I noticed he became eager to get his mail, and that he suddenly began to sign most of the stuff and send it back."

For a while there were other signs that Gray may have been emerging from his shell and his reclusive lifestyle. When the Memphis Chicks, the team that catapulted Gray to fame in the 1940s, returned to the Southern Association after an absence of seventeen years, he surprised everyone in Nanticoke when he accepted an invitation to throw out the first ball at Tim McCarver Stadium in Memphis. "There were about ten-thousand people there, and they gave me a standing ovation," he said in a rare acknowledgment of public adulation. "They drove me around in a Cadillac and everything. It was really something."

It was also extremely rare. In subsequent years, Gray declined all invitations—to oldtimers' games, to card shows, to anything. "I don't want to go anywhere," he said in the summer of 1993, hinting that he felt that people still perceived him as some kind of a freak, rather than one of the most remarkable baseball players of all time. "Pete's been getting a little more friendlier, mellowing a bit," said Chet Pientka, his former mailman. "But he won't go anywhere because he thinks people want to take advantage of him—that they think of him as a freak."

What Gray always seemed unable to comprehend was that most people aware of what he had accomplished as a baseball player admired him immensely, particularly for his determination and perseverance. Many have wondered, given Gray's achievements as a one-armed player, how good he might have been if he had had two arms. Would he have been far better? Perhaps even achieved higher greatness? The question was posed to the old "One-Armed Wonder" on a gray wintry day in Nanticoke. "Who knows?" he said. "Maybe I wouldn't have done as well. For one thing, I know I probably wouldn't have tried as hard and practiced as much as I did, and I probably wouldn't have had the same determination to make it to the big leagues."

But he did and, for one season at least, Pete Gray demonstrated conclusively that he belonged, not as some sideshow freak, but as a "One-Armed Wonder" of incredible talent, capable of performing wondrous feats on a baseball field.

CHAPTER 10

ANN WALTERS

More than a few of Ann Walters' classmates at Bloomfield High School in Connecticut envied her lifestyle. During her first two years, she spent September and October attending classes at the school, playing soccer, and running on the cross country team. Then from about November 1 until April 1, Ann would attend the Killington Mountain School at one of America's best known ski areas in Vermont. There, she would take typical high school courses and spend hours every day practicing as a member of the U.S. Junior Development Ski Team, the cream of the crop of the country's most promising young skiers. In April, Ann would return to Bloomfield High, where she would be reunited with her hometown friends and spend the last three months of the school year, while also competing on the girls' track team. Even though she was away during most of the school year, Ann was so well-liked that, by her sophomore year, she had already been elected a co-captain of both the girls' cross country and track teams.

In the eyes of many of her friends, Ann Walters was leading a glamorous, even charmed, life and enjoying the best of two worlds. Her future was very bright indeed. By the time she was fifteen, Ann was ranked in the top ten among the nation's junior girls' slalom ski racers and had already spent part of the 1983 summer, when she was only fourteen years old, attending an elite ski camp at Mount Hood, Oregon, at the invitation of the U.S. Ski Team. A year earlier, when she was thirteen and in middle school, Ann was already receiving high-quality ski poles and goggles at no charge, a sure sign that ski accessory manufacturers regarded her as a very bright skiing prospect.

For Ann Walters, the future could hardly have looked brighter. Savoring it all with pride were her parents, Nancy and Richard Walters, avid skiers themselves who had started Ann skiing at the age of four, with their two older children, John and June, also good skiers. Although both John and June developed into outstanding skiers, good enough to become ski instructors in Colorado, it was Ann who became the skiing star of the Walters' family. From the beginning, as a young child, she showed extraordinary talent during the family's frequent ski trips to Vermont where they had a vacation home. By the age of nine, she was competing in junior races and winning most of them. And by the time she turned twelve, the U.S. Ski Association was well aware of her skills, inviting her to become a member of the Junior Development squad the following year while spending the winter at Killington Mountain.

Yet, Ann Walters was hardly a one-dimensional athlete. As a teenager, she was a good soccer player, an outstanding distance runner, and a fairly good tennis player. But it soon became evident that if she were to go anywhere in sports on the international level, it would be in skiing.

One of her coaches at Killington Mountain, Chuck Hughes, ran an "in-snow" camp in the Austrian Alps for three weeks each summer. Invitations to the camp were cherished, and Ann was ecstatic when Hughes invited her to join some of her Killington teammates and some other high-ranking American junior skiers in Austria in August of 1985, following her sophomore year at Bloomfield High. As at Mount Hood, she would again have an opportunity to ski with, and compete against, some of the best young skiers in the country. Like their youngest daughter, her parents were thrilled, even though it meant that, again, as during the past two winters, they would not see Ann for weeks. But they knew how much the trip meant to her, and they encouraged her to go. In early August she flew to Austria on the longest trip of her young life.

Ann loved the camp and the exquisite beauty of the Austrian Alps in August, a dazzling blend of warm weather and soft skiable snow. It also gave her an opportunity to see her Killington friends again and meet other young skiers from throughout the United States. Unlike at Killington, although practice sessions were rigorous, the camp was more vacation than grind.

For early August, the skiing was spectacular.

So much so that even after practice sessions, Ann and other campers went out on "fun runs" down the mountain, freewheeling sessions that she came to love. On Saturday, August 3, at the end of her first week at the camp, Ann was out for a fun run with a few friends when, suddenly, racing down the mountain she lost control, somersaulted through the air, and landed on her back. Lying in the snow, Ann felt no pain as her friends rushed to her side. But at the same time she was unable to move. "Someone get this off me!" she yelled out as she pounded on her left leg. "Ann, that's your leg," one of her friends said, terrified at the thought of what might have happened. "Then it dawned on me," she recalled nine years later. "I had no feeling in my legs. And I knew what that meant. I was paralyzed."

Calls for emergency assistance immediately went out, and in minutes, a toboggan with a stretcher arrived. But a decision was made not to move Ann Walters, not in her condition. Instead, a call was put in for a medical helicopter. Then a "snowcat" was summoned to clear a space on the mountain for the helicopter. All the while, Ann's friends, stunned but trying to conceal their fears, tried to console her. Eventually, the helicopter landed and, after she was placed aboard in a stretcher, it took off for a hospital in Innsbruck, the site of the 1976 Winter Olympics.

A few hours later, about noon in the Eastern United States, six hours earlier than in Austria, the phone rang at the Walters' home in Bloomfield. Richard Walters answered. The voice on the other end was that of Chuck Hughes, the camp director, whom the Walters knew from Killington. "Richard, Ann's been hurt in a fall while skiing," Hughes said. "I'm sorry to tell you this, but her back is broken. She's in the hospital, but she's not in any danger."

Richard Walters blanched. "How did it happen and where is Ann?" he asked, stunned by the news.

"She was out skiing with some other kids this morning— it wasn't a regular training session—when she somehow lost control and flipped over in midair," Chuck Hughes replied. "Ann's in a hospital nearby, and they're taking good care of her. They say there are no other injuries."

"We'll come right away," Richard Walters said. "But just hold on a second while I tell Nancy."

By then, Nancy Walters, sensing that something was wrong, had come into the living room. "Ann's been hurt in a skiing accident," Richard Walters said softly to his wife. "Her back's been broken, but otherwise she's all right. Chuck Hughes is on the phone."

A chill went through Nancy Walters' body, and she felt faint. "Oh my God, no!" she exclaimed. "Oh no!"

"Chuck, tell me exactly how to get to the hospital and where we should fly into," Richard Walters said, resuming his conversation with Hughes.

"You've got to fly to Zurich first and then take a shuttle to the airport near here," Hughes said. "I'll get more specific directions and call you back in a few minutes. When you get here, I'll have someone pick you up at the airport and take you to the hospital."

That evening, Richard and Nancy Walters, both in a state of disbelief, left Kennedy Airport in New York for Zurich, Switzerland. From Zurich, they flew in an eight-seater to Innsbruck.

By mid-Sunday morning, they were at the hospital. As they walked into Ann's room, she looked up from her bed, her face brightening. "Mom! Dad! How did you get here so fast?" she asked, smiling.

"We booked a flight out of JFK as soon as we could after Chuck called and told us what happened," Richard Walters said, comforted by his daughter's smile. "How are you, honey?"

"I guess I could be better," Ann answered, again with a smile.

Both Richard and Nancy Walters then took turns hugging their daughter, deeply saddened by the sight of her in bed, but relieved to an extent by her cheerfulness and sense of humor.

"I couldn't believe how it happened," Ann said, anticipating the question. "We were just making a fun run when I suddenly went out of control and went flying through the air. Then I couldn't feel anything, and knew something was really wrong. The ironic part is that I've had a lot of far worse spills than this one. But, don't worry; I'm going to be okay."

Richard and Nancy Walters looked at one another. Before going in to see Ann, they had been told by doctors that she had fractured her thoracic spine and severed her spinal cord in the accident. That meant, doctors told the Walters, that Ann would probably never walk again—that she was paralyzed from the chest down. *Yet she thinks she's going to be all right,* they both thought to themselves.

For the next ten days the Walters stayed in Austria, spending practically all of their time at the hospital, and as much of it as possible with Ann, whose spirits remained high. Finally, in mid-August, the three of them flew back to the United States together. Ann was taken directly to St. Francis Hospital and Medical Center in Hartford, about ten miles from their Bloomfield home, where she stayed for ten days. She was then transferred to the Newington Children's Hospital, just south of Hartford, a renowned medical facility for young people. There, in the hospital's Acute Rehabilitation Unit, she would spend three months letting her injuries heal and learning the new skills she would now need for facing life without the use of her legs. As for most people, and particularly teenagers, who have suddenly lost their mobility, it would be a long and daunting process.

But it was during her stay at St. Francis Hospital in Hartford that the hard reality of what had happened and the overall outlook hit home. "At first, I thought I was going to recover," she said at her apartment in Champaign, Illinois, shortly before receiving her masters degree from the University of Illinois in the summer of 1994. "I was home and I felt sort of 'Okay, let's get this nightmare over with and get back on my feet again.' Then it sank in—the realization that I probably wasn't going to walk again. I tried to be strong during the day when my parents and others came to visit me, but at night, quite often, I'd cry myself to sleep."

At the Newington Children's Hospital she struggled while learning how to get in and out of a wheelchair, how to maneuver through tight spaces, how to maintain her balance, and even how to get up after a fall. She did extremely well. "I'm sure she was helped by the upper body strength and coordination she had gained from her years of competitive skiing," said Patti McVey, a physical therapist who worked closely with Ann.

After Ann had been at the hospital for a few days, Lori Bates, another physical therapist, who was aware of her sports background, told her about the hospital's active sports program. "She encouraged me to get involved, but I was hesitant to do so," Ann recalled. Finally, she agreed to

accompany Bates to the gym. There, Ann saw children,
including a number of teenagers about her age, whirling
about in wheelchairs. Some of them weaved in and out of
cones, others sprinted and raced, while some practiced
balancing on their back wheels, a method used to mount
curbs and steps. "At first, I thought, 'This is not for me.' But
then as I kept watching, I said, 'Hey, wait a minute! Maybe
I ought to give all of this a try.'"

The following day, Ann Walters was zipping around the
Newington Children's Hospital gym, and before long, she
was racing with teenagers her age and with some of the
older children. "I began to realize that wheelchair racing
was sport, too, and I realized that if I wanted to stay involved
with sports, this was going to be the way. Sports had always
been a big part of my life, and I certainly didn't want to let
go. Then when I began to hear about all of the wheelchair
competitions, I thought, 'Hey, even though I'm in a
wheelchair, I can still compete after all.'" Soon Ann was
taking part in wheelchair races at track meets and doing
well. "It was great. I was back into sports again and
competing against some very good athletes."

During her stay at the Newington Children's Hospital,
there were occasional dark moments. "I'd get frustrated
because I couldn't do some very simple things. And there'd
be angry minutes, but they never lasted long. I would keep
things—different frustrations—bottled up inside. Then I'd
blow up when my mother was visiting me. And I'd cry. It
wasn't fair to take it out on her, but I felt she could relate to
me more than anyone else. That's the way it usually is
between mothers and daughters."

But her mother recalled that her occasional flashes of
anger were the result of frustrations, not self-pity. "It was
never a case of 'Why me?'" Nancy Walters said. "And Ann
never got depressed, at least when we were there. I think if
Ann had gotten hurt some other way, say, in a car accident,
it would have been harder for her to accept. But that fact
that it happened while she was doing something she loved,
skiing, may have made it easier."

There were frequent visits from friends, including
members of the track and cross country teams. "Ann was
never upset when we visited her," Kevin Over, the coach of
both teams, said. "The first thing she'd ask was 'How is the

team doing?' And when we'd ask about her, she'd say, 'Don't worry about me; I'm going to be okay.' We really didn't have to work at cheering up Ann. She'd cheer us up. That's the way she was."

Apart from her family, Ann's most frequent visitor was Tony Kapsis, a teacher at Bloomfield High. "Ann's mother and I had gone to the University of Hartford together, and I also knew her father," Kapsis said. "But I hadn't had Ann as a student and had only a nodding acquaintance with her. But I had watched her play soccer, and I had been very impressed with her spirit and determination. She'd really catch your eye. Then I heard at the start of the school year in September of 1985, after Ann's accident, that she needed a tutor in psychology, which I taught. Well, I certainly could feel a sense of empathy towards her because we lost our daughter to cancer when she was fourteen, and so I volunteered to tutor her after school."

For three months, three times a week, Kapsis tutored Ann at the Newington Children's Hospital, and then, after she had been discharged, for a month at her home in December before she returned to school in January of 1986. "I'd find Ann in up and down moods at the beginning, but after that she was always up. My daughter had been in Boston Children's Hospital, which was loaded with courageous kids, and one thing I learned was that you can't over sympathize with them. So as a teacher, I tried to be stern and yet loving. And I think it worked, even though I could be strict. Once, she cried after I gave her back a paper that I had marked 'unacceptable' with a notation that 'you can do better.' She finally understood and, after that, her work improved. Then when she came back to school, I had Ann in a psychology class and she excelled, getting an A."

While at the Newington Hospital, and after her discharge, Ann took part in an innovative Functional Electrical Stimulation program, wherein her paralyzed leg muscles received computer-controlled electrical stimulation. The electrical stimulation enables the leg muscles to contract without receiving signals from the brain through the spinal cord. At first, the stimulation only permitted her to raise her legs up and down. But after three months, the treatment had strengthened her leg muscles to the point where she could pedal a stationary bicycle for up to forty-five minutes.

To Ann, her parents, and staff members at the hospital this was an encouraging sign, but no guarantee that Ann Walters would ever walk again.

Throughout her stay at the Newington Children's Hospital, Ann kept her emotions bottled up except, occasionally, when her mother was around. This concerned her doctors. One day, she finally broke down in front of one of her doctors, sobbing because of the knowledge that, after almost three months at the hospital and despite all of the treatments, she still could not walk. "Ann, I think you're finally ready to go home," the doctor told her, glad that she had finally shown some emotion relating to her paralysis. This was normal behavior, and it meant that she was ready to leave the hospital.

In January, Ann returned to Bloomfield High. "It was a little scary at first because I didn't know how people were going to react," she said. "But everybody was great. They treated me just like in the past. And I guess it was because I really hadn't changed. I was the same person I had been before the accident, except that now, I was in a wheelchair."

That year, 1986, as she became more accustomed to the wheelchair, Ann competed in a number of wheelchair races, winning many of them. In the spring, she helped Kevin Over with the track team. After all, she felt, she had been elected a co-captain before the accident and it was only right that she got involved, even if her duties mainly consisted of clocking the team's runners and exhorting them on during meets. She came back to help out again during her senior year with both the track and cross country teams. "Ann was a terrific leader and very popular with her teammates," Over said. "And her presence after the accident helped tremendously."

In December of her senior year at Bloomfield High, sixteen months after her accident, Ann Walters went skiing for the first time. It was at a clinic for disabled skiers in Ohio. Only now she skied on a mono-ski, wherein the skier sits on a seat with outriggers which are mounted on a single ski. Her parents accompanied Ann to the clinic and could not help but notice the gleam in her eye as she made her first run down a hill. Later that winter, she also went skiing at Lake Tahoe, Nevada, with Lori Bates, who had been one of her therapists at the Newington Children's Hospital.

After graduating from Bloomfield High in June of 1987, Ann felt she was ready for some serious wheelchair sports competition and entered the National Junior Wheelchair Championships in Princeton, New Jersey in July. Not only did she dominate the events in her class, winning ten gold medals in a variety of track and field events, but she was voted the Outstanding Junior Female Athlete, the highest honor bestowed on an athlete at the event. It was a remarkably auspicious debut in national competition.

That summer she also began playing tennis again with her mother, taking advantage of the two-bounce rule that is accorded wheelchair players. Getting more and more involved in road-racing, she also finished first in races in Falmouth, Massachusetts, and Newport, Rhode Island. She also continued her arduous training regimen, which included thrice-weekly Nautilus sessions, swimming, weight lifting, and both distance and sprint sessions in her racing wheelchair which weighs fifteen pounds, about half the weight of a conventional wheelchair.

By late summer it had become obvious that Ann Walters was already developing into one of the nation's leading wheelchair racers and was a strong prospect for the U.S. Paralympic Team in the 1988 Olympics in Seoul, South Korea, a year away. In the meantime she decided to enroll at the University of Illinois, which has one of the best wheelchair sports programs in the world. This decision was based considerably on a recommendation from Tom Foran of West Hartford, Connecticut, a top wheelchair racer, who had been instrumental in getting Ann into road-racing and who knew the Illini wheelchair track coach, Marty Morse.

At Illinois, Ann, always looking for a new challenge and not satisfied just performing for the women's wheelchair track team, also went out for basketball, and she made the women's wheelchair team. What made that particularly remarkable is that Illinois traditionally has one of the best women's wheelchair basketball teams in the nation and, secondly, that Ann Walters had never played basketball, either when she was able-bodied or after her accident. But her natural athleticism, quick reflexes, mobility, and fierce competitiveness soon made her an integral part of the Fighting Illini women's team. So much so that she received the Most Improved Player Award both after her first and second seasons.

"Ann was a very tenacious player," her coach, Brad Hedrick said. "And the stronger the opposition, the better she played. What made it all amazing was that she had never played basketball before coming to Illinois."

Ann Walters' schedule at the University of Illinois during her freshman year was mind-boggling. Besides playing for the basketball team and racing for the women's wheelchair track team, she carried a full load of courses. That meant hours of practice virtually every day, plus a heavy load of homework (as everyone who has been through it knows, the freshman year in college is the hardest), lifting weights, working out on Nautilus equipment, and preparing for the 1988 Olympics in Seoul, at the end of her first year at Illinois.

Competing in her first Paralympics, against the world's best wheelchair athletes, Walters, in only her second year of major competition, was outstanding. She won a gold medal in the 4x400-meter relay, a silver medal in the marathon, and bronze medals in the 200- and 800-meter races. "It was incredible; I never expected to do so well in my first Paralympics," she said. Thereafter, her career as a wheelchair athlete really took off, both in the U.S. and abroad.

Besides starring on the wheelchair track and basketball teams at Illinois, Ann also was a standout in the classroom. She made the Dean's List and won the coveted George Huff Award, given for excellence in academics and athletics, three years in a row, and her major, kinesiology, the study of human movement, was hardly an easy one. During her varsity career, the women's wheelchair basketball team won the national collegiate championship every year. As a senior, she was named to the national tournament all-tournament team. How good is the Illini wheelchair women's basketball program? Well, in 1988, when Ann Walters was a freshman, seven of the team's eight players (Ann was the exception, opting to participate in racing) tried out for the U.S. National Paralympic Basketball Team, and six of them made it, while the seventh was named an alternate.

While taking a full course load and playing two sports, Ann also traveled extensively during her six years at the University of Illinois (she earned a master's degree after completing her undergraduate work), winning nine ten-kilometer (6.5 miles) races and ten marathons throughout the U.S., in England, and Holland, including four consecutive

Chicago Marathons from 1990 through 1993. During one remarkable stretch in 1992, the Illini sports star won four marathons (26 miles, 285 yards) in four consecutive weekends. "And in each one my time got faster and faster, with my fastest in Chicago at one hour, forty-four minutes, and twenty-nine seconds," she recollected. (The world record for women wheelchair marathon racers in 1994 was one hour and thirty-four minutes, only ten minutes faster than Walters' time in the 1993 Chicago Marathon. But in wheelchair marathon racing, ten minutes is not necessarily a significant amount of time, since, as Walters pointed out, "with a tail wind behind you, you can really fly.")

But even for a superbly-conditioned athlete like Ann Walters, four marathon races in four consecutive weekends was a bit too much. "After the fourth one, in Chicago, I was really wiped out," she said.

Earlier that year, in the summer of 1992, Walters achieved one of her greatest honors when, following an outstanding performance in both track and field events, she was named the Outstanding Female Athlete at the National Wheelchair Championships in Salt Lake City. That summer, she also competed in her second Paralympics as a member of the U.S. team in Barcelona. Unlike in 1988 though, Ann did not win any medals. "I had a great year overall, but just didn't do that well in Barcelona," she recalled. "For one thing, they changed the classifications, which made it more difficult for me. But I'm not complaining because, with the changes, it's actually better." Initially, Ann only had to contend with other wheelchair athletes who, like herself, had been paralyzed from the chest down. But, with the change in classifications, she had to compete against athletes with less severe disabilities.

Like many, if indeed not most wheelchair athletes, Ann Walters preferred to take part in competitions that also involved able-bodied athletes. That has been the case in several U.S. Olympic Festivals. "It gives us a chance to watch them (able-bodied athletes) compete in their sports, and they in turn get to watch us. The best part of it all is mixing with the other athletes, who realize we train as hard as they do and who treat us as athletes, not wheelchair athletes. That means a lot to us."

Having been helped by so many people during her sports

"comeback," Ann Walters has been determined to help others
in turn. While at the University of Illinois, where she received
a bachelor of science degree in Kinesiology in May of 1992
and a master of science in the same field in August of 1994,
along with a master's degree in Sport Management, she
served as a student teacher at both a high school and
elementary school in Champaign; was an instructor at a
rehabilitation hospital in Birmingham, Alabama; served as a
sports counselor-instructor at a University of Illinois Summer
Junior Wheelchair Sports Camp for five years; took part in
several coaching clinics; and was a graduate assistant in the
Department of Recreation and Athletics in charge of special
events at the university.

"Good coaching in both road-racing and basketball has
enabled me to achieve the success I've had, and I want to
give something back," she said, while preparing for the
National Wheelchair Championships in Alaska, in 1994.
"And I think the fact that I was a strong athlete as a skier
made the transition to wheelchair sports easier for me. But
I've had to work hard, too, lifting weights three times a
week and sprinting and racing between eight and twenty
miles a day when I was preparing for a competition."

Reflecting on her injury and her paralysis, Ann said: "I
was only sixteen when I broke my back. But I did it while I
was doing something I loved—skiing. I'd rather it happened
that way than, say, in a car accident or some other way."

Walters disdains sympathy, even though she realizes
people, in expressing sympathy for wheelchair athletes, may
mean well. "I've never liked people looking at me and
considering me 'courageous' or 'inspirational' unless it's in
a positive way and relates to something courageous or
inspirational that I've done in a competition, like maybe
Carl Lewis would do in a race or Jennifer Capriatti in a
tennis match. Otherwise, I find it patronizing. In other
words, I don't want people looking at me and saying, 'Oh
look at how good that little crippled girl is!' I also don't like
to get cheers and hugs when I lose or to be told I did great
when I finished in tenth place and probably did lousy."

Looking ahead, Ann said she had long since come to
accept her life in a wheelchair. "I don't think about the
possibility of walking again. Why dwell on it when it may
never happen? There's tons of treatment out there and

progress is being made every day. So if it happens, and I can walk again some day, then great. But I'm not going to worry about it. And for now my life is in a wheelchair and I'm not going to complain about it."

Ann Walters has always had the knack of looking at things in a positive way. For instance, she was able to see an irony in the aftermath of the accident that ended her career as a competitive skier and as an Olympic skiing prospect.

Referring to her former teammates on the U.S. Junior Development Ski Team, she said, "I look at it this way. I got to the Olympics (in Seoul, South Korea in 1988) before any of them. It's just that I took a different route."

CHAPTER 11

JOE GLEN

Joe Glen smiles at the recollection. He had just finished fighting a three-round amateur bout in Ludlow, Vermont, in 1978, and as is the custom in amateur boxing, was standing in the center of the ring with the referee and his opponent, Bill Logan, awaiting the decision. Suddenly, to the obvious amazement of the crowd of 1,500 at the Ludlow High School gymnasium, the ring announcer intoned: "I'd like you all to know that the fighter from Holyoke [Glen] fights with an artificial leg." Many of the spectators gasped, while others let out a collective cheer. As they did, Logan, from Winooski, Vermont, looked up at the ceiling, an expression of incredulity on his face, and exclaimed, "Oh, my God!"

As if that weren't enough of a blow to Logan's ego, the referee then turned and raised Glen's right hand, signifying that he had won the decision. Even though Logan was the "home" fighter for whom the crowd had been rooting during the fight, the vast majority of the spectators, stunned to learn that Glen had fought so well with an artificial leg, cheered lustily for the visiting victor.

"It wasn't the first time that an opponent of mine and the crowd didn't know that I fought with an artificial leg, nor was it the last," Glen said years later at his home in the Sixteen Acres section of Springfield, Massachusetts. "I always wore high socks, so it was pretty hard to tell. And I guess I moved well enough so that people couldn't tell, either."

Not that Joe Glen, now in his mid-thirties, was ashamed of or had a complex about having an artificial leg. "It was just best not to let my opponents know about it," he said. "Otherwise, they could try to take advantage of it particularly in a clinch when they might try to shove you and knock you off balance. And most of the time I guess I did a good job of concealing the fact that I was fighting with a prosthesis."

The late writer, A.J. Liebling, who wrote extensively and elegantly for *The New Yorker* magazine, often about boxing, used to refer to it as "the sweet science." That may have been a nice turn of phrase, but it was a misnomer. For boxing is perhaps the cruelest and most barbaric of sports— an activity wherein the avowed goal of the participants is generally to render an opponent senseless. Ironically it has attracted some of the sporting world's noblest figures— trainers like the late Ray Arcel and Eddie Futch, both gentle and gracious men who trained fighters, many of them great champions, well into their eighties. Likewise, it has drawn into the prize ring such gentlemen-fighters as Jersey Joe Walcott, Ezzard Charles, Floyd Patterson, James J. Braddock, Michael Spinks, Jose Torres, Archie Moore, Emile Griffith, Alexis Arguello, Gene Tunney, and Beau Jack.

For many of them, boxing, if not necessarily the road to riches, was the highway to fame and a better way of life, as long as they were able to avoid punch-drunkenness, as all of the above did, or worse, death in the ring.

For Joe Glen, boxing had a different defining element when he was barely a teenager. "It really helped define me as a person," he said. "I didn't do too well in team sports, and I was usually the last one picked because of my disability. But in boxing I was on my own, and I was able to dominate others."

So it was, strangely enough, that Joe Glen who had been born without a right foot, had to turn to the most dangerous of sports with a seemingly insuperable handicap to establish an identity in sports, and in the process build up his self-esteem and confidence against able-bodied fighters, quick to capitalize on an opponent's disadvantage, whether it was a cut eye or an artificial leg. "I know it sounds crazy, but fighting in the ring was the best thing that ever happened to me."

That Joe Glen ever got into the prize ring at all—and he was to have thirty-eight amateur fights in all—was remarkable, not only because he only has one leg, but in light of the travail he endured during the first ten years of his life. Born two months prematurely on November 28, 1958, weighing three pounds and seven ounces, baby Joe had a number of severe birth defects. He had no right foot, a clubbed left foot with underdeveloped toes, and webbed fingers on both hands. So far as could be determined, the defects were caused by amniotic band syndrome, a condition that occurs in about one of every 100,000 births. As is usually the case in such births, the defects came as a surprise to Joe's parents, Frances and Joe Glen, Sr., who already had two healthy and normal daughters.

Little Joey, as he was called by his parents, was to spend much of his early years at the Shriners Hospital for Crippled Children in Springfield, not far from the family home in Ludlow, where the Glens had moved when Joe was two. Over a period of ten years, he was to undergo numerous operations to correct the clubbed foot and webbed fingers. At fourteen months he was fitted with his first prosthesis, and by the time he was ten, he was able to go home for good after having spent anywhere from six to eight months of each year at the Shriners Hospital.

"Joey spent so much time at the hospital and became so accustomed to the surroundings that when he came home he was always playing doctor," his mother recalled. "He was very observant, and had watched and listened to the doctors and nurses at the Shriners Hospital very closely. And when he would play, he'd always be using a lot of medical terms and talking about various medical procedures. Then, by the time he came home for good, he would pretend to be a doctor—even dressing like one in surgery—and use make-believe medical instruments for his 'operations.' And he told us many times that, when he grew up, he was going to be a doctor."

Playing outside was much more difficult. "I was in the hospital so much that it was difficult for me to make friends in the neighborhood," Glen said. "And then when I finally came home for good, I had to start a whole new chapter in my life, and it wasn't easy."

Particularly when it came to team sports. "I wanted to play baseball, soccer, football, and just about everything else, but not everyone wanted a kid with one leg on their teams. So I was usually the last one picked for pickup games, if I was picked at all."

Usually, though, young Joe got to play, and often it was because of the intervention of his oldest of two sisters, Jean.

A good athlete, she made sure that her little brother was included in neighborhood games. "Sometimes a kid would say, 'We don't want him to play', and Jean would insist that they include me in. And if they resisted, she'd get right into their face, no matter how old they were, and demand that I play, too."

Jean Glen Merchant, the wife of a career Air Force man, recalled getting involved on behalf of her little brother. "Yes, I did fight for Joe and insist that the other kids let him play," she said. "To me, it just wasn't fair that he was being left out at times because of his disability. And I'd do all I could to make sure that he was included."

To do so, at times, Jean Glen had to get rough. "I remember once this kid, who was bigger and older than Jean, didn't want me to play, and she started arguing with him," Joe recalled. "Next thing I knew she had knocked him down and was sitting on his chest, saying, 'He's going to play! Do you understand?' And I did. Other times, if Jean heard kids saying things about my disability and indicating they didn't want me in their games, she'd tell them to shut up or back off. And it usually worked."

Still, little Joe Glen was often slighted and, at times, the slights hurt, sometimes deeply.

An episode that occurred while Glen was in the fourth grade had a profound and lasting impact. It happened during a school recess. "A group of boys, including me, were organizing a soccer game," Glen recalled. "There was an odd number of boys and, one by one, everybody was picked but me. So there I was left standing on the side of the field as the rest of the kids ran out to play. As they did, one boy turned to me and called out, 'You can't run. You can't dribble the ball. You can't do anything.' It was painful. But as I walked away from the field, I vowed to excel at some sport—I had no idea which one or how I would do it—but I resolved to do it. And then as time went on, I realized I wanted to get involved in a sport where one athlete dominates the other with power, beating him soundly, with no question as to who the winner is."

Meanwhile at home, young Joey Glen had changed career dreams, going from would-be doctor to would-be soldier. His father had been in the Army during World War II and, after hearing him talk about his experiences in the military, little Joe decided that he, too, would someday go marching off to war in some faraway place. "He got so wrapped up in being a soldier," his mother said, "that he'd wear a camouflage uniform, carry a canteen and toy gun, wear a backpack, and set up a pup tent."

His sister, Jean, recalled her little brother marching around the house in his army uniform. "He was obsessed with being a soldier," she said. "Then one day our father took him aside and told Joe that, because of his missing foot, he could never go into the Army. That broke Joe's heart."

Still, there was no stopping little Joe Glen. If he couldn't be a soldier, he'd do something else, and he'd do it well.

"No matter what happened," Frances Glen said, "Joe was always a happy, good-natured boy. And, in spite of his physical defects, he tried everything, and he always wanted to be treated as an equal. For instance, we used to ski at a place called Hemlock Hill, not far from where we lived, and one day I took Joey up for a lesson and sat in the car waiting. Then at one point Joey was coming down the hill with his instructor, practicing snowplowing when he fell and his prosthesis came off. I could see that the instructor was flabbergasted, and later when he had gotten down to the bottom, I heard him say to someone, 'See that kid up there that I'm instructing? He's got an artificial leg!' I had to laugh because I realized that Joey hadn't told the instructor about his leg. He didn't want to be treated any differently than anyone else. That was Joey."

Though he endured little taunting in general, young Joey Glen was self-conscious about his artificial leg. "I'd always wear long pants, even on hot days in the summer," he said. "But one very hot day my mother convinced me to put on a pair of shorts, although I didn't want to. She said, 'Joey, put on shorts, like the other kids. It's too hot for long pants.' So I did. But then when I went out, some of the other kids came over to me and right away, wanted to touch the artificial leg. So I ran right home and put on long pants again."

In retrospect Glen finds some incidents, which were embarrassing at the time they occurred, somewhat amusing years later. "I remember once when I was late for a class and started running down the hallway in school when I tripped and fell and my prosthesis flew off—the shoe, sock, everything," he said. "Well, there was a girl nearby, and she saw it happen and couldn't believe her eyes. She let out a scream, and then she fainted, right there in the hallway. I can't say that I blame her."

There were also poignant moments. "Joe loved to swim," his sister, Jean, recalled. "But to do so, he had to take off his prosthesis, and he was self-conscious about doing it. So he'd usually go over to a corner of the pool, then take off the prosthesis as inconspicuously as possible, put it on the edge and then jump in. He didn't want anyone to see him take the leg off."

A turning point for young Joey Glen came during the winter of 1971. Muhammed Ali, back from the fistic exile imposed upon him for refusing to go into the Army during the Vietnam War, was about to fight the reigning champion, Joe Frazier, at Madison Square Garden in New York City. It became one of the most ballyhooed fights of all time, and twelve-year-old Joey Glen became fascinated by it all. He knew his father had boxed some while in the Army, and one day leading up to the Ali-Frazier fight in March of 1971, he asked his dad if he could show him how to box. *Why not?* Joe Glen, Sr., thought to himself. So Glen dug out an old duffel bag, filled it with rags, and father and son had a punching bag, which Glen hung up in the basement. First, he taught his son how to jab, then how to throw a right cross, an uppercut, and finally, combinations of punches, one after the other in rapid-fire style. Pounding away at the homemade punching bag, with his dad looking on, little Joe Glen suddenly realized, *this is it. This is what I want to do in sports. I want to be a boxer.* Meanwhile Joe Glen, Sr., noticed one thing right away, that for a twelve-year-old, his son had one heck of a left hook.

It wasn't long after that that Joe Glen, Sr., got an old set of boxing gloves out of the attic and began to spar gently with his son. "He loved it, that was easy to see," Glen said many years later. "And he could really throw that left hook."

Between sparring with his dad and punching the homemade bag, little Joe Glen quickly became enamored with boxing. It was the one-on-one sport that he had been looking for, the one where one athlete dominates the other. Enthused because of the realization that he just might be able to excel in boxing, Joey Glen began to challenge friends to box with him in a makeshift ring he had set up in his backyard the following summer. "I beat all of them, easily," he said. That November, when Joey turned thirteen, his father gave him what turned out to be a much-cherished birthday present—a speed punching bag to complement the full-sized homemade bag he had been using since the previous spring.

Having run out of friends as boxing opponents—"after a while, they didn't want to box with me anymore," Glen recalled with a smile—he had to look elsewhere for competition. He found it that fall and winter at the Springfield Boys Club. "My father had taken me to see Eddie 'Red Top' Owens, who was a high-ranking light heavyweight at the time, fight at the Springfield Civic Center. And a short time later, I read in the paper that Owens was starting up a boxing program at the Springfield Boys Club and talked my father and mother into letting me get involved."

That was no easy task. "It was one thing for Joey to be hitting the punching bags in the basement or boxing with his friends in the yard," Frances Glen said. "But to get involved in a boxing program under a professional fighter, well, I didn't like that idea at all." Even Joe Glen, Sr., the old Army boxer who had taught his son the rudiments of the sport, was not crazy about the idea. "I didn't want Joe to get into any actual competition, and he was only thirteen years old," Glen said. "It's a dangerous sport and we were concerned about Joe trying to box with his prosthesis."

But his parents relented, mainly because young Joe Glen let them know, with considerable passion, what boxing had meant to him—how it raised his self-esteem and boosted his confidence. "I'm good at it, too," he told them as he pleaded his case. "And all the kids around here and in school know it."

That was a telling point and Joey Glen's parents knew it. For he had not done well in team sports where, when he played at all, he felt unsure of himself and ill at ease, knowing that he was usually not wanted as a teammate. "Okay, Joe," his father finally said. "But be careful, and try to be as good a defensive fighter as you are with that left hook."

So, at the age of thirteen and weighing 110 pounds, Joe Glen became a boxer at the Springfield Boys Club which, ironically, is directly across the street from the Shriners Hospital for Crippled Children, where he had spent most of the first ten years of his life. From the outset he was in his element, savoring the head-to-head competition, the noise, the excitement of it all. Early on, Owens, who in the early 1970s had been a ranking light heavyweight, took a liking to Glen. "I think I was the hardest worker in the boxing group, and I think Eddie saw my burning desire. Once in a while, he would even spar with me. He took it easy, of course, but I did pretty good, and it gave me a lot of confidence."

Before long, during the winter of 1972, Joe Glen, at the age of thirteen, began to compete in three-round bouts as a Junior Olympian. "I won my first couple of fights easily, and then Eddie began to bring in some tough kids from Springfield. He'd say to them, 'Hey, I got this white kid from Ludlow who's pretty good. You think you can beat him?' Some of them were pretty good, but I beat them. I remember once I fought a kid who wouldn't take his wool hat off—I guess because he thought he could beat me easily, knowing I had an artificial leg. Well, that got me mad, and I caught him with a left hook and his hat flew off his head and he went down, with the hat landing on him. That was the end of that. Another time, Eddie brought in this guy who looked much older than the kids I was fighting. And I said to him, 'Eddie, this guy is kind of big and he's also kind of old,' and Eddie said, 'Don't worry; you can take him.' Later I found out that the guy was twenty-one years old. And I was only thirteen!"

For four years, from the age of thirteen until he was sixteen, Glen was a member of the Springfield Boys Club boxing team under Owens. Fighting first as a flyweight, and then as a bantamweight and lightweight featherweight, he was virtually invincible, winning all seventeen of his fights as a Junior Olympian. Certainly no fighter trained harder— mornings, before going off to Ludlow High School, Glen did three miles of roadwork with an artificial leg no less, and then topped off his early day workout by skipping rope and doing five hundred sit-ups, usually while exercising with weights. If ever Joe Glen was to lose a fight, it wasn't going to be because he was not in shape. Ironically, sit-ups, and not boxing, earned Glen his greatest measure of fame at Ludlow High when, as a sophomore in 1974, he broke the school record for sit-ups when he did 1,500 of them in fifty-six minutes. Not only did he break the old record, he demolished it—by 381 sit-ups.

By then, Glen felt he was on his way—not as a sit-up record-breaker, but as a boxer. "The boxing did wonders for me. I know it's a tough sport, but it gave me my own identity."

During his sophomore year, Glen switched over to the Holyoke Boys Club, about fifteen miles north of Springfield whose boxing facilities were far superior to its Springfield counterpart. There he was to work under Pat Bartlett, a veteran trainer who had trained and managed Eddie "Red Top" Owens when he fought as an amateur. "Eddie brought Joe to me one day and told me he was good fighter," Bartlett recalled. "He also told me that Glen only had one leg. I must say I wasn't too excited about training a one-legged fighter, but I said to Eddie, 'Well, let's see what happens!' Well, I soon saw that he could move very well. So well that I was absolutely amazed. And he was a very hard worker who listened and paid attention. He also had a heart as big as a lion, and a murderous left hook. There was no doubt he could fight.

"A lot of the guys he fought didn't know that he had only one leg. And he did his best to conceal it by wearing high socks that went up over his prosthesis. But the fighters who did know about it tried to take advantage by pushing him backwards and trying to knock him off balance. But Joe was both tough and strong and he could handle such tactics, but sometimes he would fall down, either when he was pushed or by falling accidentally. And even though Joe had the artificial leg, he didn't fight flatfooted as you might expect, he moved. He worked harder than anybody else, and he didn't fear anybody. And he could really take a punch."

In 1975, while a sophomore at Ludlow High, Joe began his post-Junior Olympic boxing career as a full-fledged amateur with no age restrictions. Fighting in the Western Massachusetts Golden Gloves tournament in Holyoke in the 135-pound lightweight novice class, Glen got off to an auspicious start, scoring a second-round technical knockout over Tony Knox of Springfield. Glen eventually lost a decision in the quarterfinals, but by then had become a huge crowd favorite because of his aggressive style, courage, and, of course, his devastating left hook.

Two months later in his next fight, which also turned out

to be his most memorable, Joe Glen wasted no time in unloading that wicked left hook which had become his Sunday punch. Appearing on a boxing card in Wethersfield, Connecticut, that included former champions Jersey Joe Walcott and Willie Pep, Glen was matched against Art Crespo of Meriden. After the opening bell both fighters exchanged jabs in the center of the ring. Crespo threw another jab, which Glen eluded. As he did, he unleashed a left hook that caught Crespo flush on the jaw, sending him to the canvas unconscious, but uninjured. By the time the referee finished counting ten, the total elapsed time of the fight was seventeen seconds, which made it one of the quickest knockouts in boxing that year, or any other.

Neither of Glen's parents were in the crowd that night. They rarely saw their son fight. "I went once, when Joe was just starting again," Frances Glen said. "I didn't like it at all, and I never went again." Yet she conceded that boxing had helped young Joey. "After he got into boxing, he had more confidence in himself; it definitely helped his ego."

Joe Glen, Sr., the old Army boxer who unwittingly had gotten his son interested in boxing, went to see him fight a number of times. "I just kept hoping he wouldn't get hurt," said his father, who retired in the late 1980s after working in the shipping department of a Ludlow factory for many years.

Throughout high school and during his first two years at Springfield College, Joe Glen, Jr., kept on boxing—"the Fighting Schoolboy" who, fighting with one leg, was better than most of the boxers with two legs that he faced. By 1976, Glen, then seventeen, had moved up to the welterweight class (147-pound maximum weight) and again reached the quarterfinals of the Western Massachusetts Golden Gloves tournament before losing. By now Glen had begun to think seriously of eventually becoming a professional fighter. His hopes began to dim when the following year, 1977, he lost in the quarterfinals of the Golden Gloves for the third year in a row. "If I couldn't get past the quarterfinals of a regional Golden Gloves tournament, I began to doubt whether I had any future in boxing. But that's not why I was boxing in the first place. I was doing it because I loved it. I didn't set out to become a professional fighter."

Just about the time he began to doubt himself as a fighter,

Joe Glen, now nineteen and a sophomore at Springfield College, majoring in physical education, launched his most successful year as a boxer. Fighting as a middleweight at 156 pounds, Glen won ten of twelve fights. One of his victories was against an inmate at the maximum security Connecticut State Prison in Somers, Connecticut.

"I'll never forget that fight because the guy I fought, Herb Fernandez, was the best fighter I ever faced," Glen said. "He boxed my ears off for the first two rounds (all amateur fights are three-rounders). He would jab me and then run, and I couldn't catch up with him. But then in the last round, with time running out, he caught me with another jab. But as he did, he dropped his head and I was able to nail him with a left hook and knocked him cold. The inmates loved it. They didn't necessarily root for *their* fighters. They just wanted to see a good fight, and I kind of think they appreciated a good puncher more than a good boxer. So I guess I won them over." For Joe Glen, it was to be the high-point year of his fistic career. And he was only nineteen years old.

Disenchantment set in early the following year during the Western Massachusetts Golden Gloves tournament, which Glen had skipped in 1978 after only reaching the quarterfinals three years in a row. Given his outstanding year in 1978, Glen now a light heavyweight at 171 pounds, seemed poised for an even better year. "As a light heavyweight, I figured to do even better because as you get into the heavier divisions, as a rule, the fighters are heavier and slower, and you don't have to move as much. That, of course, would be better for me."

Glen never had a chance to prove that thesis in the 1979 Golden Gloves tournament, an event in which he had become a big crowd favorite. Even though he had fought in three previous tournaments in the last four years, Glen was barred by one of the tournament's ring doctors because of his disability. Incredulous, Glen appealed, pointing out that he had reached the quarterfinals in his three previous appearances, was no less fit in 1979, and was even a better fighter, as his 1978 records attested. The ring doctor, in barring Glen, also said he had been informed by an anonymous source that Glen had been knocked out during a fight two weeks earlier at the Connecticut State Prison.

"I was told that one of the other coaches was afraid that I would beat his fighter in the tournament," Glen said years later at his home in Springfield. "So he went to the ring doctor and, besides pointing out that I fought with a prosthesis, said that I had been knocked out in a non-existent fight in Somers. And they went along with him."

During a subsequent meeting on the matter in advance of the tournament, Glen produced a letter attesting to the fact that he had not fought in Somers two weeks earlier, as he had been charged. A referee and several others also testified on his behalf, all of them pointing out that Glen had been boxing for eight years without any problem relating to his disability. But the tournament committee and three ring doctors ruled that Glen could not take part in the Western Massachusetts Golden Gloves event. "I was devastated," he recalled. Months later, after Glen had hired a lawyer, the Massachusetts Boxing Commission and the New England Amateur Boxing Federation both ruled that Glen should have been permitted to participate in the tournament and reinstated him as an amateur boxer.

For Joe Glen, the incident marked the beginning of the end of his boxing career. "I didn't fight at all that year or the next, going to school full-time and working as a security guard at the Westover Air Force Base. But I kept doing roadwork and my sit-ups, and stayed in shape just in case I decided to fight again, which I thought was unlikely."

Not really, because by 1981, after graduating from Springfield College, Glen, his competitive fires burning again and yearning to box, returned to the gym to spar. Before long he decided to launch a comeback at the age of twenty-two. But Glen's two-year absence from the ring was a detriment, and the old fire was no longer there. "I just wanted to fight again, but something was missing," he reflected more than a decade later. Glen had three fights during his brief comeback, losing the first two by decisions, while fighting as a middleweight again at about 156 pounds.

His last fight was in Northampton, Massachusetts, against a promising fighter from Hartford named Elliott Williams, who would eventually turn professional. Glen heard that Williams would be a formidable foe; little did he realize how formidable. Not only could Williams box well, he could also punch. Glen's only hope was to land his vaunted left hook. But, as in his previous two comeback bouts, he was unable to do so, and against Williams he was outclassed.

"Early in the second round, the guy really clocked Joe—knocked him cold," said Matt Mullaney, who refereed the fight as he had a number of Glen's other bouts, and had even sparred with him, although he was twenty-five years older. "When Joe got up, I put an arm around him and said, 'Joe, this is your last fight. If you want to stay in the game, I'll see to it that you become a judge.' Joe looked at me, right in the eye, and said, 'Okay, Matt. I won't fight again.'"

He never did, retiring from the ring with a 29-9 record, with his intellect and health intact.

"Joe had a colorful career, but he knew when to get out," said Mullaney, a veteran referee at amateur and professional fights throughout New England, who had fought professionally in the 1960s. "Joe was a student of the game, and he had great determination. And I knew he would make an excellent judge, which he did. He was a good boxer—and he had to be, considering his handicap. And that left hook of his was tremendous."

After graduating from Springfield College, which offers one of the best physical education teaching programs in the nation, Glen became a gym teacher at a state juvenile detention center. Here he established and ran a boxing program for about three years until it was eliminated as, eventually, was his job for budgetary reasons. Later, Glen became a correction officer at a juvenile detention center in Westfield, Massachusetts. He continued to keep his hand in boxing as a ring judge in New England. Glen also turned to writing, authoring a book about training entitled, *Conditioning for Amateur Boxing*, which covers virtually every possible aspect of training and conditioning. Given his own arduous training regimen, his fierce dedication, and his success as an amateur boxer, Glen was well-qualified for such a project.

Beyond his boxing career, sports continued to play an important part in Glen's life. He built a gym in the basement of his home, where he worked out daily with weights and various Nautilus equipment and, at 170 pounds, bench pressing three hundred pounds. A speed bag which hung from the ceiling, was the only reminder of Glen's boxing career. "Every once in a while, I'll hit it a few times, but my wife uses it more than I do," he said. Glen also played tennis occasionally with his wife, Susan, a social worker, whom he married in 1987.

Still competitive, Glen got into road racing for a while, competing in a number of five-kilometer (3.1 miles) races in the Springfield area. "I averaged about eight minutes a mile and usually came in dead last," he recalled with a laugh. "But I had fun." Even after he stopped competing in cross country races, Glen kept on running, doing three-and-a-half miles around a reservoir three times a week in under thirty minutes.

Since 1989 his main sport has been bike-riding, not just recreational bicycling, but competing in "century" events that cover one hundred miles. In fields that have ranged from thirty-two to 136 racers, Glen never finished lower than ninth. He consistently improved his time, from seven hours and forty-five minutes in his first race to under seven hours in 1993.

At times while he was a teenager, there would be dark moments. "I'd be out doing roadwork at 5 o'clock in the morning, running three miles with an artificial leg," he recalled. "Sometimes it hurt, and I'd say to myself, 'Why me?' But I got over that and stopped feeling sorry for myself early on." If anything, Glen believed, he might not have done as well as a boxer, and in sports in general, if he had not been born without a right foot. "Maybe I wouldn't have worked as hard as I did. Maybe I wouldn't have had the same drive and wouldn't have tried as hard."

Glen had to try extra hard for more reasons than one. "No one ever took it easy on me during a fight," he said. "They'd see me come gunning for them right from the start, and so they treated me just like they would any other fighter. And in some cases, where my opponents knew I had an artificial leg, I think they might have tried even harder because they didn't want to lose to a one-legged fighter, not that I necessarily could understand that. But on the other hand, maybe I would have reacted the same way if I ever fought a one-legged fighter."

Because of his strenuous lifestyle, Glen went through about forty artificial legs by the time he was thirty-five. For many years he was in and out of hospitals, especially as a child and as a young man, undergoing a number of operations. Those experiences, in the long run, served him well, both from a medical standpoint and in giving him a perspective about his handicap.

"When I'd been in the hospital, particularly the Shriners, I'd see kids and other young people a lot worse than me. Some would be in full body casts. And I remember seeing one kid who had no arms or legs. Then there was the kid I saw who was blind and had no hands. One day his mother was killed in an accident while driving to the hospital to see him. And then a few days later, the kid's father died in another accident while driving to her funeral. My situation couldn't compare with someone like that.

"I've been able to do just about everything I wanted to do, and I never considered myself handicapped. But it was the boxing that really helped me establish an identity and prove that with one leg, I could do well in a very tough sport."

CHAPTER 12

JONATHAN SLIFKA

Wheeling to his left, literally, the second baseman for the West Hartford Red Sox reached down, scooped up the ball, then flipped it to the other second baseman, Mike Slitt, who in turn threw it to first just in time to get the batter out.

Two second basemen on the same team? Yes, indeed— one positioned directly behind the bag and the other in the conventional position between first and second base. Nobody on the opposing teams ever complained about the arrangement, though, because the Little Leaguer stationed back of second base, Jonathan Slifka, was playing his position in a wheelchair and would have found it impossible to cover it on his own. When he was at bat, a special accommodation was also made for young Slifka during his three years in the West Hartford Youth Baseball League. As he batted from his wheelchair a designated runner stood alongside, taking off for first base when Jonathan hit the ball, which was most of the time. During his last season with the Red Sox, Jonathan collected twenty-two hits, including a home run, and batted well over .300 as his team went 10–2 before losing in the championship game. True, opposing pitchers tossed the ball underhanded to Jonathan, but that seemed only fair, since he was batting from a wheelchair.

"None of the other teams ever complained about that, even though we had an outstanding team," said Mark Wertheim, who was the coach when Jonathan played with the Red Sox, "and a lot of the opposing players even rooted for Jon when he was at bat. He made good contact at bat and came through with some crucial hits, particularly during his last season. As a matter of fact, he hit better than most of the other kids on the team. And he fielded well, too. He's a well-coordinated little guy who could scoop up grounders, caught the ball well, and had a pretty good arm. He's an amazing kid."

That Jonathan Slifka could play baseball with his peers, and play it well, is truly remarkable, since he was born with spina bifida and is unable to walk. (Spina bifida is a neurological impairment resulting from an undeveloped spinal column. Babies born with the affliction have a hole in the spine, where the spinal cord covering has failed to form.) After "retiring" from baseball at the age of eleven, Jonathan went looking for another sport's challenge and found it in tennis, where he developed into a strong player, good enough to beat able-bodied players while playing the game in a wheelchair. Beyond the world of sports, he also demonstrated considerable musical talent as the youngest, and only non-adult member of his church choir, and as an accomplished flutist in the high school band. Since he was thirteen years old, Jon, who turned seventeen on June 13, 1994, has also been a volunteer at the St. Mary Home in West Hartford, Connecticut, where he visits, chats, and plays cards with patients many years older in an effort to cheer them up.

To say the least, Jonathan has made his parents, Robert and Janeace Slifka, and his older brother, Scott, very proud. "He is a very stubborn kid, which I think is what gives him his spunk and drive," Janeace Slifka said. "In our town, it seems that Jon is the one paving the way for other kids. He is always the first—the first kid in a wheelchair to attend all of the regular schools, the first kid in a wheelchair to play Little League baseball, the first kid in a wheelchair to play team tennis for his school, and the first wheelchair kid to attend a camp really meant for able-bodied children."

All of this from a teenager who could not even sit up until he was seventeen months old and did not start to crawl until almost a year later. "For a while, we thought he would never crawl," his mother recalled. "Then one day, while I was on the phone with my mom, Jon, who was two-and-a-half at the time, spotted a potato chip on the floor and got up on all fours and crawled to it. I was so happy that I started screaming. Meanwhile, Jon had a big grin on his face. He has been crawling since and can get up and down stairs, and in and out of the bathtub unassisted. This has prevented him from having problems like scoliosis (a curvature of the spine) and sores from sitting all the time.

"When he was a little tike, around two, three, and four, Jon was an avid fan of the super heroes like Superman and Batman, who were his favorites. My cousin bought him a cape that reversed to either one of those super heroes, and Jon wore it everywhere, always thrusting his arms forward as if to fly. It turned out that was really good for him. We found that out when he took a series of muscle tests, and the therapist noticed that his upper back was quite strong, but couldn't figure out why. When we told the therapist about some of Jon's routines, including acting out the super heroes, she came to the conclusion that his upper body strength was due to his mimicking Superman in flight."

Little Jon may have lacked mobility, but not imagination or creativity. "As a little kid he was never without a play microphone in his hand. And he would sing into the mike or pretend he was interviewing someone or was a TV weatherman. Other times he would pretend to be conducting an orchestra while listening to classical records. And he sang beautifully, often with his dad. We have some of the songs on tape and they're priceless."

What may have been the turning point in little Jon's life occurred when he was six years old and attended a summer camp for able-bodied children at the University of Hartford, in West Hartford. "Even though our area is saturated with camps, you haven't lived until you try to find organized summer activities for a handicapped child," Jon's father, a financial consultant, said. "Having had no success in finding anyone's arms opening at the prospect of a wheelchair-bound camper with continence difficulties, we decided to try to get him into the Summer Place, the camp at the University of Hartford, which was run by the school's men's basketball coach, Jack Phelan. They'd never had a handicapped child before, but no issue was raised, and we pointed out Jon's needs and specifications. So Jon turned out to be a trailblazer at the camp, as he was to be in a number of other areas.

"At this stage, Jon hungered to be normal, and at the camp he was, participating in almost every activity in his wheelchair, and in some cases out of it. For example when his group mates got on the gym floor to be put through their paces by Phelan, Jon got out of his wheelchair to be there with them. And when they assembled at the end of the day, Jon was there on the floor with them again."

It was at the summer camp that Jonathan first got caught up in sports. Since Phelan was a basketball coach, basketball was naturally the main sport. Before long, Jon was shooting hoops from his wheelchair and even learning how to pass and dribble. "He fell in love with basketball," Janeace Slifka recalled. "The only problem was that, after the camp, when we'd ask him what he wanted to be when he grew up, he would say, 'An N.B.A. player.' That broke our hearts because, obviously, that was not going to be possible. But we wouldn't say anything to Jon about it. Eventually, he came to the realization that would be extremely difficult, to say the least, so when we would ask again what he hoped to be, he would say, 'The first disabled N.B.A. player!' We knew then that he was becoming more accepting of his disability, but still was refusing to acknowledge that it had any limitations, which was great."

Jonathan Slifka earned several awards during his six weeks at the summer camp, and every time he did, he would crawl across the gym floor to receive the award from Phelan, who treated him like every other camper. During the final closing ceremonies on the last day of camp, after announcing the top achievement awards, Phelan, the big, gruff-talking coach, announced that there was a special award "to someone who exemplified courage and determination to achieve beyond his abilities—to someone who was not blessed with the gifts and skills that others take for granted, but who, despite that, has shown up and participated to the fullest." Then Phelan called out Jonathan Slifka's name. Taken aback at first, little Jon, three-feet tall and thirty-five pounds, began his usual crawl forward on his hands and knees. As he did, everyone, campers, counselors, and parents stood and applauded. Phelan, the six-foot two-inch, 220-pound coach, who at times took on the demeanor of a Marine Corps drill sergeant, got down on his own hands and knees and crawled to meet Jon as the cheering and applause grew. The gruff but compassionate coach hugged Jon and gave him his award. Jonathan's parents were moved to tears, as were many in the University of Hartford gymnasium that August day.

"Never have I seen that saying better epitomized," Robert

Slifka was to say later. "'No one stands so tall as he who stoops to help a child.'" Later, the Slifkas thanked Phelan for his overall concern for Jonathan, his acceptance of him as just another camper, and, in particular, his symbolic gesture of getting down on his hands and knees. The coach said, "After watching what he did for six weeks, I was just coming up to his level."

That same summer, Jonathan, eager to pursue his interest in music, took a recorder class at the camp. At the suggestion of his instructor, he began to take lessons on the flute, an instrument he soon came to master, playing it at church and later, in the band at the William Hall High School in West Hartford. When he was sixteen, Jon and two friends formed a trio, and after practicing every Saturday afternoon for six weeks, played a piece by the Austrian composer Joseph Haydn during a Father's Day program at the St. Peter Claver Roman Catholic Church. "They were really terrific, and we were so proud," Janeace Slifka recalled. By that time, Jon had also joined the "Cruisers" wheelchair track team at the nearby Newington Children's Hospital, where he had undergone therapy for years. "Jon got involved with the Cruisers when he was six after we realized he wanted to be part of a team, wearing a uniform, and competing against others and not just his own time. It did him a world of good, and he kept at it, racing with the Cruisers for four years until he was ten."

It was at that age, while the Slifka family was vacationing in Hawaii, that Jonathan got involved in tennis. "Jon was sitting in his wheelchair watching Bob play with our other son Scott, who is three years older than Jonathan and a very good athlete," Janeace Slifka said. "The pro at the courts came over and asked Jon if he played, and when he said he didn't, the pro asked if he'd like to give it a try. It turns out that the pro—I wish I remembered his name—taught wheelchair tennis. As it developed, he gave Jon a few lessons and Jon was hooked on the game."

It was a turning point for Jon because he soon realized that tennis was a sport he wanted to play over the long haul. By then he was playing Little League baseball, but he knew deep down inside that he'd only be able to play the game for a few years. Another turning point occurred the fall of that same year when Jon met Ivan Lendl to pose for a

Connecticut March of Dimes poster. When Lendl found out about Jon's interest in tennis, he did something about it. Shortly after they met, Ivan encountered Brad Parks, the founder of the National Foundation of Wheelchair Tennis, at a sports convention in Atlanta and told him that he had this friend back in Connecticut who wanted to become a tennis player. Lendl also told Brad Parks that if Parks helped Jon, he in turn would help promote wheelchair tennis. So a deal was struck. "The next summer, Brad contacted us and Jon went to one of his camps in San Diego and loved it," Janeace Slifka said.

Though confined to his wheelchair, Jonathan, at the age of ten, became a three-sport athlete—racing with the Newington Children's Hospital Cruisers, playing Little League baseball, and playing tennis.

As a baseball player, little Jon Slifka was a sight to behold, particularly in the field, scooping up balls hit his way and then flipping them to nearby teammates for relay to the appropriate base. That Jon played baseball at all was a complete surprise to himself and to just about everyone else, including his parents. "I never expected to play," he recalled. "Mr. Wertheim [Mark Wertheim, his Little League coach] is a friend of my parents, and he had asked me to help him with the team when I was nine, keeping score and so on, and he even gave me a uniform. Before the season started, I'd bring my glove to practices and practice with the other kids, but I didn't expect to play."

But on opening day he got the call. "Mr. Wertheim called me over before the game started and said, 'Jon, get out there on second base.' I couldn't believe it because he had never asked me if I wanted to play. But I had on my uniform, and I had my glove, so I hustled out there in my wheelchair."

Jonathan's parents were incredulous when they saw him take the field. "It was a real shock," Janeace Slifka said, "because Jon had never played in an actual baseball game." It was hardly an auspicious debut, but that was understandable, considering how young Slifka found himself wheeling after ground balls lunging down with his glove, and trying to scoop them up. Even when he was able to do that, he then had to throw the ball to his nearest teammate, an extremely difficult chore at best.

"He didn't do well at the start, and he'd get upset after

games," Janeace Slifka said. "But he kept at it, practicing as much as possible, and he stuck it out. It was obvious that he was very happy to be part of the team."

For Bob Slifka, seeing his crippled son positioned at second base was heartwarming. But it also was a cause for concern. *How can he possibly stop a ball?* Slifka asked himself. *And if he possibly can, how can he possibly throw it? And how in the world is he going to hit the ball batting in a wheelchair?*

"Jon's always loved sports, and in recent years he had expressed an interest in playing on a town team, and one of the main reasons is because his brother, Scott, is such a good athlete," Slifka said. "But we'd have to say to him, 'Jon, they don't take kids in wheelchairs.' But, suddenly, there he was, out on the field in an actual game. It was great, but it was also kind of frightening. But for Jonathan it's always been important to succeed in whatever he tried. And fortunately he has great drive and is very competitive. He takes losing very hard. And I knew he did not want to look bad playing baseball or anything else."

Though he endured a disappointing first year in the West Hartford Youth Baseball League, Jonathan Slifka was not discouraged. He came back with the Red Sox for a second, and then a third year. Largely because of all of his practicing and his unremitting determination, he got better and better. His coach, Mark Wertheim, never lost faith in him. Fiercely competitive, little Jon also got spunkier and spunkier, to the point where at times his competitive fires almost got the best of him. "If he didn't like a call, he'd argue with an umpire and then even come over to me in the bleachers to complain," his mother said. "I'd tell him to be quiet and concentrate on the game, but it didn't always work."

Even though the Red Sox were one of the best teams in the league, opposing pitchers kept lobbing the ball over the plate so that Jonathan could hit it. "They realized that he could hurt them at bat, but they wanted him to do well," Mrs. Slifka recalled. "It was an interesting lesson in human nature." Of all of his hits during his three-year Little League career, the most memorable for little Jon was his only home run. It was far from being a prodigious shot; rather, it was a ground ball that hopped through the first baseman's legs and wound up against the fight field fence. As soon as the ball left Jonathan's bat, his runner, Ben Harris, took off for

first, then second, then third, and finally for home as
Jonathan, still holding his bat in his wheelchair at home
plate, screamed at the top of his lungs, exhorting his runner
on and then high-fiving him as he crossed the plate. Rarely,
if ever, did a home run mean as much to a player as it did
that day to Jonathan Slifka.

Thereafter, young Slifka concentrated on tennis, hitting
for hours with able-bodied friends at Elizabeth Park, near
the Slifka's home in West Hartford, or with his father at the
Hartford Golf Club. By the time he was thirteen, Jonathan
had won a national tournament for junior wheelchair tennis
players in Mission Viejo, California. Flushed with that
success, he then took tennis lessons at the Bloomfield and
Farmington Valley racquet clubs in the Hartford area.

Inspired by their son's athletic accomplishments and
convinced that there were other wheelchair-bound
youngsters eager to get involved in sports, the Slifkas opened
a free junior wheelchair tennis training and sports camp at
the University of Hartford, which donated space for the
camp. Such camps were common in the West, like the one
run by Brad Parks that Jonathan attended, but unknown in
the East. To raise money for the camp, which opened in the
summer of 1991, the Slifkas organized a fundraiser at the
Hartford Golf Club. The star attraction was Jon's friend Ivan
Lendl, who rallied with anyone contributing $1,000. There
were enough takers to make the camp so successful that it
has become an annual event, held each August, at a site in
the Hartford area. Lendl, who lives in Connecticut, also
took part in subsequent fundraisers, as did actor Gene Wilder,
who also lives there. Among those who hit with Lendl at
the fundraisers was his favorite practice partner, the former
.300 hitter, Jonathan Slifka.

By the time he got to Hall High School in West Hartford,
Jonathan was ready for a new challenge, his toughest yet—
trying to make the powerful Hall High boys tennis team,
which was in the midst of a sixty-seven match winning
streak. "First, I went to the coach (Jim Solomon) and told
him I wanted to try out," Jonathan, four-feet ten-inches
and, seventy pounds at the time, said. "He told me that he
had no problem with that." This posed a possible dilemma
for Solomon. "I knew they used a two-bounce rule in
wheelchair tennis, so I asked the C.I.A.C. [the Connecticut

Interscholastic Athletic Conference] if they had such a provision for a wheelchair player, and they said they didn't. But I certainly felt that Jonathan had the right to try out for the team. Then if he was going to make it, I would have had to try to persuade the C.I.A.C. to let him compete."

However, that was not necessary since Jonathan, though allowed two bounces on shots, lost all four of his matches against other aspirants for the powerful Hall squad, which had not lost a match in four years. As a result, he did not make the team. "I really thought I might be able to make it," Jonathan said, "but I didn't do very well in my matches." Still, being cut from the team was hard to take. "I was calm about it when Coach Solomon told me about it. But when I got home, I lost it and cried, but not for long. I realized that I wanted to be judged like everyone else, and that I still had three years left in high school."

As it turned out, Jonathan was an integral part of the Hall varsity boys' tennis program that first year after all. "Though I cut him, I realized that Jonathan was a very special and courageous kid with considerable tennis talent, whom we'd like to have around," said Solomon, an English teacher at Hall High who started coaching tennis there in the early 1970s. "So I asked him if he'd like to come out and warm up the players before home matches and then chart some matches for us. And I was glad when he agreed to do it."

Jonathan was touched by the coach's offer. "He was very nice to ask me, and I told him I'd be more than willing to do it." Then as the Hall team powered its way to another highly successful season, young Slifka was on hand at every home match, warming up members of the varsity. Maneuvering his wheelchair with swift dexterity, Jonathan returned the able-bodied Hall players' shots with a strong forehand and slice backhand, which were more than enough to get them ready for their matches. "We loved having Jonathan around," Solomon said. "He's a courageous kid and a very good role model."

But warming up members of the boys' varsity, while good experience and satisfying to a degree, wasn't quite enough for young Slifka. "I'm going to work hard on my game during the summer, and I'll be back out for the team next year," he told the coach at the end of his freshman year at

Hall High. He was, and this time he made it as a member of the junior varsity team. "We hadn't had a J.V. team in the past, but decided to have one in 1993 because I felt it was wrong to cut so many players, including a lot who were good enough to play on the varsity at most high schools in the state," Solomon said. For Jon Slifka and a number of others, that was good news. "I always liked the idea of playing on a team," Jonathan said. "So I was really glad when Mr. Solomon decided to have a J.V. team."

Playing singles, Jonathan lost his first match. But he played well and was competitive, and he was far from being discouraged. In his next match he accomplished a wondrous breakthrough, beating an able-bodied teenage opponent while playing in his wheelchair, yet he kept the victory in perspective. "He wasn't a very good player, and I don't think he had played much tennis," Jonathan said later in discussing the match. Nevertheless, he had proven that he could do what he was convinced he could do—be competitive against, and even beat, able-bodied tennis players his age.

There were to be other victories over other able-bodied tennis players at Elizabeth Park in West Hartford and while playing at the Watkinson School in Hartford, to which he transferred after spending two years at Hall High. By then, too, he had his first girlfriend. All the while, he still played his flute, sang in the church choir, and when he found the time, did some volunteer work at the St. Mary Home, playing cards with and cheering up patients much older than him.

Reflecting on his youngest son's extremely difficult first year of life, Robert Slifka said: "Jon endured several operations that first year, including one to close the hole in his spine where the covering for the spinal cord had failed to form. This was to prevent spinal meningitis, which is virtually fatal in these cases. Janeace and I would go visit Jon together in intensive care. And the sight of that little body attached to all the monitoring devices was heartbreaking. But the perils that awaited Jon were of a more gradual nature. To be honest, considering the problems that had been spelled out to us, we were torn and didn't know whether to pray for Jon to live or die. But eventually, after so many different operations and surgical procedures, Jon got better and better. And as he did, we became determined that he would be treated as normal as possible, and that he would have to adapt to the world the way it was and not the way we wanted it to be."

Jonathan Slifka did exactly that, going to camp with able-bodied kids, attending public schools in his hometown, playing the flute in the Hall High School band, singing in his church choir, demonstrating that he could compete with, and even beat, "normal" teenagers in tennis, and even scooping up ground balls and batting over .300 in a wheelchair.

CHAPTER 13

DAN KELLY

Even though he would have rebelled at the term, it would not have been incorrect to have called Dan Kelly a "Big Man on Campus" at Robbinsdale Armstrong High School in Plymouth, Minnesota, a suburb of Minneapolis. After all, he was vice president of the five-hundred-member senior class in 1994, a member of the student council, captain of the boys' varsity swim team, a volunteer at the high school career center, a swimming coach for visually-impaired youth, a part-time worker at radio station KQRS, and a member of the aquatic club. Despite all of those activities, Dan maintained a 3.7 grade point average during his senior year.

Outside of Armstrong High, Dan had more than his share of other interests, too. He played the drums avidly, liked to ski, devoured science fiction books, and on Friday and Saturday nights, liked to go the movies with friends or get together with them at their homes or his own in Golden Valley. Regional school board members were so impressed with Dan Kelly that they selected him as a student representative on the board.

True, there may be many more young people as active in and out of school as Dan, but the chances are that none of them is blind.

Dan Kelly has been legally blind since birth, a victim of retinitis pigmentosa which also led to the blindness of his father, Todd. Until he was about eight years old, Dan could read extra-large type, but since then he's had to rely entirely on Braille. His dad, a teacher and computer programmer whose father was also blind, was able to read headlines and enlarged type until his mid-teens when he became totally blind.

"Blindness has not stopped me from doing what I wanted to do in the past, and it will not stop me in the future," Dan Kelly said before enrolling as the first blind student ever at Gustavus Adolphus College in St. Peter, Minnesota, in late summer of 1994.

Of the many highlights in Dan Kelly's extraordinary life, the greatest perhaps, was his selection as the youngest (sixteen at the time) of fifteen blind athletes named to the 1992 U.S. Paralympic Swim Team that represented the United States in the Summer Olympics in Barcelona, Spain. At the time, Kelly held the world record for the one-hundred-meter backstroke, his strongest event. At Barcelona, given his young age, his performance was outstanding as he captured four silver and two bronze medals. His parents were on hand to see Dan compete in front of as many as 8,000 spectators.

"Standing on the medal platform in Barcelona at the 1992 Paralympic Games is an experience that will be etched in my memory forever," Kelly said later. "My performances proved to me that if you work hard enough with discipline and set goals for yourself, you can achieve all that you want. In my case, I practiced two hours a day, six days a week, leading up to the games. And along the way I had to sacrifice a lot of time away from my friends. But I decided that the end goal of medaling in the Paralympics outweighed the hard work and minor sacrifices I had to make."

At Barcelona, Kelly was competing against the world's best blind swimmers. Back home in Minnesota, he competed year-round against sighted swimmers, both in high school and in amateur meets during the spring and summer. As a senior, Kelly was unbeaten in the backstroke and won twenty-five races overall in a variety of events.

More often than not he won his freestyle and medley events (in which a swimmer has to use four different strokes—freestyle, backstroke, breaststroke, and butterfly) while also winning most of the relay events in which he was entered. "Sometimes it's hard for me because I don't know where the other swimmers are in a race," he said shortly before his graduation from high school. "I just keep trying to go as fast as I can all the time. And the coach [Tim Buckley, his high school coach] helped by yelling a lot."

Dan's mother, DeeDee, also helped her son during his high school meets, and not just by yelling. So that they know they are nearing the end of the pool, blind swimmers are permitted to take advantage of "boppers" at either end of a pool, wherein someone reaches out and touches the swimmer with a long pole that has a soft object, such as a tennis ball, attached to it. "My mom usually did it at one end and the coach at the other," Kelly said. Nevertheless, there were times when he crashed into swimming pool walls.

Unlike other swimmers, Kelly counts his strokes so that he always knows, or at least has a good idea, where he is during a race or in practice. He also relies on pool "waves" from gutters along the edge of a pool and from lane lines to let him know how close he is to the side or to a lane line.

As good as he was in high school, Kelly expected to be even better in college, where he realized that competing against sighted swimmers would be more difficult. But then again, Kelly had done so well against the best blind swimmers in the world in Barcelona, most of whom could, and in some cases did, hold their own in strong college competition.

Besides knowing when to turn, swimming in a straight line is another major concern for a blind swimmer. "At times, I've gotten my hand or a finger caught in the lane lines," he said. "But as a rule I follow the lines pretty well, and to do that, I've just got to swim as straight as I can."

Like many children, Kelly began swimming at the age of three. Though he soon developed into a good swimmer, he did not start competing until he was thirteen and in junior high school. By the time he got to Armstrong High he had no qualms about going out for the team. "I felt it would be a real challenge, not only for Dan, but for all of us when he came out," Tim Buckley said. "But from the beginning, he just wanted to be treated like everyone else, and there was no doubt that he was a good swimmer. He was an inspiration to everyone on the team, and if you didn't know he was blind and watched him swim, you'd never know it."

To Dan Kelly, swimming is probably the most natural sport, but not necessarily the easiest, for a blind athlete. "You have freedom of movement in the water," he said. "You can do things in the water without worrying about tripping, like you might running. And for me it's always been an escape from the normal routine of things. While I'm swimming, I work extremely hard and reach a peak, both mentally and physically."

Kelly first made a big splash nationally, both literally and figuratively, at the championships of the U.S. Association of Blind Athletes (USABA) in New York in 1991, when he won three gold medals and two silvers. That performance earned him a berth on the 1992 U.S. Paralympic Team. At Barcelona, Kelly, then only sixteen, was thwarted from capturing four gold medals by John Morgan, regarded as the best men's blind swimmer in the world. He edged Kelly out in the one-hundred and two-hundred-meter backstroke, the four-hundred-meter freestyle, and the two-hundred-meter individual medley, while winning eight gold and two silver medals overall. In beating Kelly in the one-hundred-meter backstroke, Morgan then thirty years old and fourteen years older than Kelly, also broke the Minnesota teenager's world record which he had set only six weeks earlier by twenty-one tenths of a second.

A year later, Kelly was invited to the U.S. Olympic Festival where he finished first in the one-hundred-meter backstroke and third in the one-hundred butterfly. His times continued to improve during his last two years of competition in high school as he began to look forward to the 1996 Paralympics in Atlanta.

From the beginning, DeeDee and Todd Kelly were determined to raise Dan as a normal child, despite the fact that he was born legally blind. "In the first few months of Dan's life, a doctor friend told me that, from day one, expect success for your child and never make a handicap an excuse for anything, because having a handicap was not the end of the world," DeeDee Kelly said.

A decision also was made early on to send Dan to a regular nursery school—which, coincidentally or not, subsequently hired a blind teacher's aid—and to public schools.

"Todd's [Dan's father] knowledge of the education process kept us one step ahead knowing what should be happening with Dan and his schooling," DeeDee Kelly, a paraprofessional in education, said. "His inside knowledge of the handicap was no small matter. In the years to come, we found many teachers and coaches who thanked us for giving them the experience of Dan. A few said that you get back more in terms of group cohesiveness, rather than a fear of the unknown."

The thought of sending Dan to special schools was never

a consideration. "We knew that mainstream education was the only way for us to stay a family," said DeeDee Kelly, who also has another son, six years older than Dan. "We could no more send him off to a boarding school than anything."

Little Dan adapted easily to his sighted classmates. If they could do some things he couldn't, then he in turn would accomplish feats they found overwhelming. In kindergarten, for instance, Danny Kelly was doing between 100 and 150 sit-ups in gym class—extraordinary for a five-year-old. His classmates were amazed, but not jealous. "It bolstered his own self-confidence," DeeDee Kelly said.

About that time, DeeDee and Todd Kelly bought Dan his one and only pair of glasses. He could still see a bit then, though not much. *So* they thought, *why not try glasses. What if they really did some good,* DeeDee thought. Now his classmates were excited because they suddenly thought that Danny could really see! They reasoned that he must, because he was wearing glasses, just like a few of them. But the glasses did not help a bit, and they were soon discarded.

In spite of his blindness, little Danny Kelly began to envision doing things that, in real-life, only sighted people can do. For example, when he was in the third grade, Dan and a friend whose hearing was severely impaired got together and decided to become astronauts. Or in their case, an astronaut. How? Simple. They would use Dan's hearing and his friend's sight.

If the astronaut dream died aborning, the one to become a competitive swimmer did not. When he was around seven or eight years old, Dan began to do forward and backward rolls in the center of the family living room, right in front of the television set. After a while, DeeDee and Todd Kelly caught on. Their youngest son, it turned out, was training to do flip turns in swimming which by then he was into with a vengeance. By the age of eight, he had become a prospect.

In the classroom, Danny Kelly's lack of sight proved to be no substantial hindrance. Early on he mastered a brailler, a machine with six keys which became, for Danny, comparable to his classmates' pencils and notebooks. He was always at or near the top of his class academically, and he got around on his own, with a folding cane, although more often than not, he was accompanied by friends as he walked to and from classes. A seeing-eye dog, if ever necessary, would come later. At Armstrong High, Dan Kelly did just fine without one. By March of his senior year, in 1994, with the swim season over, he began to look forward to the class senior prom. Four months later, he would be off to Gustavus Adolphus College to major in international management, with a heavy stress on Spanish, which he began studying in high school.

"I realized going into college that I had to use all of the skills that I possessed," Kelly said. "And some of the most important are organization, imagination, the ability to speak in public, and good humor, which helps offset my disability. These skills helped me get elected as senior class vice president in high school. And I remember how the students in my grade saw past my blindness and acknowledged that I would be a good representative for them." Dan Kelly did not feel that his blindness had been a big handicap by any means. "I have to adapt and sometimes do things differently," he said. "But I still can do them. So the end result is the same."

At times he even made light of his sightlessness, something he was able to do since he was a boy. Occasionally, while riding with a friend or friends, he would hand his white cane to the driver and ask him to hold it out the driver's side window. At the same time, he would ask the driver to drive especially slow, and other motorists were at times startled to see a blind man's cane sticking out the driver's side window. More often than not though, the gag evoked smiles and laughter, with the heartiest guffaws coming from Dan Kelly.

"Dan Kelly is an incredible young man," his high school swim coach, Tim Buckley, said following Dan's final season at Armstrong High. "He worked harder than anyone, and out of twenty-eight swimmers his senior year, he was the second best all-round on the team. And he's been a tremendous inspiration to his teammates who regarded him as a terrific swimmer, not a terrific blind swimmer. As a matter of fact, the other kids never thought of Dan's blindness, or certainly hardly ever. With his sense of humor and the way he acts in general, you'd never know he was blind. And in four years, I never saw him get upset at all over anything."

As a rule, swimmers competing against Dan were not

aware of his blindness, even though Buckley would lead him to the starting blocks at the edge of the pool. "But some of them would catch on when they saw the 'boppers' we had to use for Dan at both ends of the pool," Buckley said. "Sometimes a swimmer would come over to me and ask, 'What are the boppers for?' Then when I'd tell him they were for Dan because he was blind, the kids would find it hard to believe, especially since Dan had probably beaten them. And in some cases, they'd be absolutely astonished."

For Dan Kelly, his blindness was never a big deal. When he swam, he thought of himself, and hoped others would too, as a swimmer—not a blind swimmer. "I always wanted people to accept me as a regular swimmer, which I am," he once said. "My blindness has nothing to do with my swimming."

Tim Buckley agreed. "Dan Kelly is an outstanding swimmer, period. I must say that it's been a blessing for me to have coached him. He's a wonderful young man."

CHAPTER 14

NANCY OLSON

To say that sports was an important part of Nancy Olson's life as a young woman would be a vast understatement. Involved in sports from the time she could walk, Olson developed into an outstanding athlete at North Rockland High School in New York, about twenty miles from New York City. There, in the 1970s, Olson was a star on the girls' basketball, soccer, volleyball, and tennis teams, and during her first three years, she was also on the swimming team. As a senior, she batted .675 for the North Rockland High girls' softball team, was named the school's top female athlete, and was chosen to the all-county softball team.

While still in high school, Olson spent part of her summers coaching a girls' softball team in addition to playing on one herself. That experience convinced her, beyond any doubt, that she was destined to be a coach once she got out of college. And why not? She was a superb athlete, loved sports, and had already had a taste of coaching and had reveled in it. After graduating from Slippery Rock State College in Pennsylvania with a degree in health and education, that's what she became—a swimming and softball coach, and teacher at Suffern Junior High School in Suffern, New York, not far from her hometown. Away from school, she remained an outstanding competitive athlete. It was exactly how she had hoped things would turn out, and she could not have been happier.

Even when a cutback cost her her teaching and coaching job, she regarded it as a temporary setback—one that would end when the recession of the 1980s did. In the meantime, she got on as the aquatic director at the Young Men's and Young Women's Hebrew Association in mid-Westchester

County, less than a half-hour drive from where she was living in Garnersville, a few miles from the Olson family home in North Rockland. Things, she felt, could certainly be a lot worse.

It was snowing hard as she drove home after work in the gloaming of an early February day in 1983. Spring and her beloved softball seemed so far away, she could hardly wait to play and coach again. The road became increasingly slippery and, suddenly, on the New York Thruway in Tarrytown, just east of the Tappan Zee Bridge, her car and another car skidded into one another. Neither Nancy nor the other driver were hurt, and damage to both cars was slight. It was, in effect, a fender-bender, but she and the driver of the second car, after pulling their vehicles onto the shoulder of the highway, got out to exchange information. As they did, a police radio car pulled up and parked to the rear of Nancy's car, his red overhead light flashing.

As the two drivers and the state policeman discussed the accident, another car went into a skid on the highway and crashed into the police car. Catapulted forward by the impact, the police radio car slammed into Nancy Olson, pinning her against the back of her own car and severing both of her legs above the knee. During almost eleven hours of microsurgery at Bellevue Hospital in New York City, doctors reattached both legs and, for at least a while, it appeared that the delicate surgery had been successful. But then infection set in and less than a month later, Olson lost both legs.

Suddenly, at the age of twenty-six, life seemed to be over for Nancy Olson. "I was devastated," she said. "Here I was always so active in sports—the shortstop on the girls' team who would hit the home run to win the game. And now, I felt, I wouldn't be able to do anything—play sports, coach, teach, do anything. I just couldn't believe it."

Olson spent most of the next year in the hospital, mostly at the Institute of Rehabilitative Medicine at the New York University Medical Center in New York. Early on, someone at the Institute, aware that Olson had been an outstanding athlete, suggested that she think of returning to sports. "How?" she asked. "I've lost my legs."

But her therapists told her how there was a virtual plethora of sports for wheelchair athletes, such as wheelchair racing, tennis, and basketball, and that as a natural athlete, she no doubt would quickly adapt to whichever ones she took up.

Nancy Olson felt embarrassed. Here she was a former physical education major in college, who knew an awful lot about a lot of sports but nothing about sports programs for the physically disabled. "When I thought about it, I realized that that was amazing and embarrassing," she said.

"Actually, as I was to find out, sports for disabled people is nothing new, and wasn't even new when I got involved in the mid-1980s. It's only new to most able-bodied people or to somebody like me after my accident. Sports for the disabled has been around for a long time; it's just that it's grown so much. I just wish that I had learned something about it when I was studying phys-ed in college."

Now, during her rehabilitation, Nancy was being asked if she wanted to get back into sports as a wheelchair athlete. It was not a difficult decision. "I decided to do it—to get back into sports as a participant, and not just as a coach, which I started to do again in the summer of 1984, coaching softball. It certainly made sense, since my whole life had been oriented towards sports. I had lost my legs, true, but I was still basically the same person as before the accident."

While continuing her rehabilitation at the Helen Hayes Hospital in West Haverstraw, which is named for the late actress who lived in nearby Nyack, Olson got involved in wheelchair racing. One of her first events, appropriately enough, was the Helen Hayes Classic, a ten kilometer race. The winner in the women's wheelchair division? Nancy Olson.

In 1985 she turned to wheelchair tennis. "I really missed playing tennis," she said, "and wheelchair tennis is tennis. It's also a sport that I can do with my friends, since you don't have to have wheelchair players to play with."

Soon, Olson was hooked on wheelchair tennis, entering tournaments and faring well, even though she was new to the game. "I picked it up quickly, and hitting with my old able-bodied friends helped," she said. "And I loved the challenge of it."

Wheelchair tennis participants in the United States alone now number in the thousands. Olson's innate athleticism enabled her to rise rapidly. All of the weightlifting during her long rehabilitation helped immeasurably, producing power in both her ground-strokes and her wicked slice serve. Her reflexes, always lightning fast, remained as quick as ever.

By 1987, only her second year as a regular tournament player on the National Foundation of Wheelchair Tennis Grand Prix circuit, Olson was ranked third in the United States in women's singles. She rose to the number two ranking in 1988, and from 1988 into the mid-90s was ranked first in the nation. Further, by 1993 she was ranked third in the world, her highest international ranking at that point. By then, Olson had already beaten the world's number one ranked player, Monique Vandenbosch of Holland. Vandenbosch got even, though, in the 1992 Paralympics in Barcelona, Spain, when she edged Olson in a three-set singles match in an early non-medal round. Olson was one of two women players representing the U.S. in the Paralympics tennis competition, which was being held as a medal sport for the first time.

Playing on the wheelchair tennis circuit at the top level, as Olson has done, is a full-time job. To prepare for Barcelona in 1992, Olson had to give up her job with the Rockland County Social Services Department. And, like professional players, the top-ranked wheelchair players rely on coaches to help improve their games. In Olson's case, she has had a number of coaches and also has several sponsors. Prize money, slow in coming in wheelchair tennis, has been minimal. "In 1993, I was ranked first in the country for the fifth year in a row, yet only made about $3,000 in prize money," said Olson who moved to Florida in 1993 so that she could spend more time working on her tennis game and also because of the availability of more players, both in wheelchairs and able-bodied.

By 1994, Olson, thirty-seven, not only was beating the world's best women wheelchair players, but playing in several tennis leagues in Florida for able-bodied players. "Strictly doubles. I'm not quite ready for singles against good able-bodied players," she said in late April of 1994 before leaving for Japan to take part in a wheelchair tournament. This meant that Olson had to return shots after the first bounce, and would not be able to avail herself of the "two-bounce" rule that prevails among wheelchair players.

"Wheelchair tennis had opened up the whole world to me—a whole new world of opportunity," she said. "For one thing, there's been the travel. I've been to England, France, Spain, Belgium, and Holland, and I'm sure I'll play in some other countries before I'm done. And I've met so many great people during my traveling. To say the least, the sport has been very, very good for me, not only because of the competition and travel, but because it's helped rebuild my own self-confidence."

As a teacher, coach, and eventually, wheelchair athlete, Olson has touched many lives, as both friends and strangers alike were drawn to her plight following her horrifying accident. Months after the accident, a man she had never met began a fundraising drive to collect money to buy Nancy a specially-equipped car that she could drive. The fundraising drive eventually raised $36,000, far more than was needed for the car, which the auto dealer in Scarsdale, New York, as a gesture on Olson's behalf had marked down considerably.

Though he had never met Olson, Joel Erenberg, who began the fundraising drive with a goal of raising $10,000, knew a lot about her. At the time of her accident, his son was taking swimming lessons from Olson at the Young Men's and Women's Hebrew Association in Scarsdale, New York.

"Nancy had made a very, very positive impact on my son and the other kids she taught," Erenberg said after the money was raised and he finally got to meet Olson. "There is an inner strength within this woman that is unlike anything any of us have ever seen before. Her spirit, right from the beginning was, 'I am going to overcome this.' And in every sense of the word, she has."

CHAPTER 15

THEY ALSO PLAYED THE GAME

For every coddled, pampered, and overpaid professional athlete, forever whining about some trivial ailment, there is someone, somewhere, who because of a disability, never had the opportunity to make it to the big-time in sports.

Ken Daniels would have loved to have made it to the National Football League. Any chance of that happening ended when Daniels lost his left leg to cancer while he was a freshman at Rosary High School in St. Louis, but that didn't stop Daniels from kicking extra points and field goals from as far out as thirty yards.

Daniels kicked with his good leg. By contrast, another place kicker, Aaron Blake, not only kicked field goals and extra points for Bremerton (Washington) High School, but also kicked off—often booming his kicks into the end zone—with an artificial right leg that was strapped to his right knee. Born without a right leg, Blake, a natural righty, opted to kick with his prosthesis rather than try kicking with his left foot. Once, during a game against Port Townsend, Blake gave it his all on a long field goal attempt, and the ball and his artificial right leg both went low and to the right. Members of the opposing team were startled, unaware that Blake kicked with a prosthetic device. Most of his teammates, though, laughed, and so did Blake. Like most athletes with disabilities or handicaps, Aaron Blake had a sense of humor that came in handy at such times in his kicking career.

Dave Reed never kicked, but he did play center and was the best blocker on the Edwardsburg (Michigan) High School football team despite the disadvantage of playing with only his right arm. Reed, who lost his left arm in a farm accident when he was ten, also played the outfield for the Edwardsburg High varsity baseball team, catching and throwing the ball in a style reminiscent of Pete Gray.

Then there were the kickers who, despite disabilities or deformities—none of them as serious as those of Ken Daniels, Aaron Blake, or Dave Reed—made it to the N.F.L.

For example, there were placekickers Tom Dempsey and Ben Agajanian. When Dempsey, then with the New Orleans Saints, kicked a sixty-three-yard field goal in 1970 to set an N.F.L. record, people marveled at the distance—and marveled even more because Dempsey did it with a toeless right foot. Incredibly, Tex Schramm, the president of the Dallas Cowboys, challenged the validity of the record kick because of Dempsey's specially-designed shoe! Schramm, who was assailed by the media and fans alike for his complaint, eventually retracted his statement. "It was a mistake and bad timing on my part," he was to say. As for Dempsey's kicking shoe, it had been examined the year before by an N.F.L. official and found to be legal. Dempsey, incidentally, had begun his kicking career as a barefoot kicker, with a piece of tape covering the stub of his foot where his toes would have been.

Some years earlier, Ben Agajanian, who played with ten teams during a nineteen-year professional career, continued to excel as one of the N.F.L.'s best field goal kickers after losing several toes of his kicking foot in a lawn mower accident.

Then there was Pat Summerall, an outstanding placekicker (who for a while also played both offensive and defensive end) first for the old Chicago Cardinals and later for the New York Giants. Summerall, who became one of the country's best-known sportscasters, overcame an even more severe handicap than Dempsey and Agajanian. He was born with a backward right foot.

"My right foot was completely turned around when I was born," said Summerall, who was born on May 10, 1931, in Lake City, Florida. "The toes were where the heel was supposed to be, and the heel was in the front."

"What could be done?" his parents asked the small town doctor who had delivered Pat. This mind you was well before the advent of specialists like orthopedic surgeons, at least in tiny Lake City, Florida. Dr. Bates knew of only one way to correct the problem. "Break the leg and turn it around," he told the Summeralls.

And that's exactly what Dr. Bates did. "Dr. Bates broke the leg when I was two weeks old at Lake Shore Hospital in Lake City," Summerall said. "Then he turned the foot around, reset the bones, and put the leg in a cast for six weeks."

The prognosis was not good.

"Dr. Bates told my mother that I might not be able to walk or run and certainly wouldn't be able to keep up with the other kids when we were playing," Summerall said.

But not only did Summerall manage to keep up with his friends as a child, but at Lake City High School he played football, basketball, baseball, and ran the 440 and threw the discus on the track team. During the summer, besides baseball, Summerall also played tennis. He played tennis so well that when he was fifteen in 1946, townspeople took up a collection so that Pat could travel to Fort Lauderdale to play in the Florida state sixteen-and-under tennis tournament. It was there in Fort Lauderdale that Summerall, with his one and only tennis racket and the only kid in the tournament wearing black Keds, won the state championship by beating Herbie Flamm, who went on to become a top-twenty player on the international circuit.

Ironically, the Lake City High School sports team doctor was none other than Dr. Harry Bates, who had delivered baby Pat Summerall, and then broken and reset his right foot.

"Dr. Bates used to marvel at what I could do," said Summerall, who during his pro career kicked 101 field goals and 258 extra points. "He told me he was amazed, he didn't think I'd even be able to run."

As it developed, Summerall did not kick in high school, but it had nothing to do with his foot. "We had a better kicker than me in Winton Criswell, whose son, Ray, later played for the Tampa Bay Buccaneers in the N.F.L."

After turning down a basketball scholarship to Kentucky, Summerall attended the University of Arkansas where, while majoring in Russian studies, he played both football and basketball. At Arkansas, he kicked only field goals while playing both offensive and defensive end.

While in college Summerall spent one summer playing first base for a St. Louis Cardinal farm team in the Class C Sooner State League. For a while during the off-season in the N.F.L., Summerall taught English and history at Lake City High for about $257 a month. An off-season job was necessary, since the most Summerall ever made in the N.F.L. was $18,000.

"I guess it's ironic," he once told this writer, "that I wound up making a living kicking with a foot that had to be turned around when I was born."

While Summerall and Tom Dempsey succeeded in the N.F.L. despite their inherent disabilities, a number of other professional athletes kept playing after being disabled during their careers. After losing part of his left leg in a hunting accident, Monte Stratton returned to pitch for the Chicago White Sox in the 1930s and finished his big league career with thirty-six victories and twenty-three defeats. Jimmy Stewart portrayed Stratton in the movie, "The Monte Stratton Story."

Another pitcher, Bert Shepard, had part of his leg shot off while he was a bomber pilot during World War II. A promising minor league pitcher before the war, Shepard still managed to return to baseball with an artificial leg and spent part of the 1945 season with the old Washington Senators of the American League.

Unlike Shepard, Buster Foley never made it to the major leagues, or even to the minors. But he had an illustrious career as a high school and college baseball and basketball player despite the fact that he lost the use of his right hand (he was a natural right hander) during a childhood accident. It was the first day of kindergarten in 1945, and little Buster Foley was anxious to get to school—so anxious that while running down the stairs of the Worcester, Massachusetts, tenement where his family lived he tripped and fell, eventually crashing through the glass section of the front door. Foley's right hand was so badly damaged that he required 260 stitches. Rather than spend that year in kindergarten, Buster spent it in Worcester City Hospital. For the rest of his life, his right hand would be of no use to him.

This disability did not deter Buster from excelling in sports as a child, and then starring in both baseball and basketball at St. Peter's High School, Worcester Junior College, and Clark University in Worcester. As a senior at Clark, the six-foot four-inch, 185-pound Foley, who was remarkably fast for his size, captained the baseball team, hit .350, and was nominated for the All-America collegiate team.

Foley, whose right arm was withered and shorter than his left, later coached baseball and basketball on both the high school and college level, and was an outstanding semipro baseball player. He also played golf and tennis, and as an athlete, became a legend in Worcester—even more than Bob Cousy, the Hall of Fame basketball player who played college ball at Holy Cross in Worcester, and then settled down there before starring for the Boston Celtics.

Like Buster Foley, Joey Upchurch also loved baseball and played it with a passion from the time he was a little boy even though he was born without a right leg. Also like Foley, Upchurch was good enough to play on the college level as a relief pitcher for the Polk Community College team in Ft. Lauderdale, Florida. A right-hander, Upchurch's fast ball was clocked in the eighties and he threw a sharp, dipping curve ball. Though he wore a fiberglass prosthesis, he still fielded his position with agility. Consistency was Upchurch's pitching trademark. In 1994, for example, he had more "saves" than any other junior college relief pitcher in Florida.

"If I hadn't watched Joey myself so often, I wouldn't believe what he's done," Upchurch's coach, Bing Tyus, said. "He has an odd motion out on the mound. Otherwise, though, you wouldn't think he was any different than other college pitchers, and he's better than most of the ones I've seen."

Scott Warren of Mobile, Alabama, also had something of an odd motion in throwing the discus, and understandably so, since he had been born without ankles. Doctors had told his parents that Scott would never be able to walk. Scott spent much of his first five years in and out of hospitals—and casts—as doctors tried to form some semblance of ankles. Competing for St. Paul's Episcopal School in Mobile in 1992, on what amounted to hardened tissue mass in place of ankles, Scott won a state discus championship with a throw of 139 feet, 1 and 3/4 inches. Scott also competed in the shot put and was a defensive lineman on the St. Paul varsity football team.

At least Scott Warren had legs. Nancy Bazanchuk of Agawam, Massachusetts, did not, but that did not deter her from competing with the girls' varsity swim team at Agawam High in the late 1980s and early 90s. That is downright astonishing since legs play such a vital role in swimming.

Because of a severe birth defect, Nancy had both of her legs amputated when she was two years old. By the following year, she was learning how to swim and quickly became very good at it. As a competitive swimmer in high school and with an Agawam Park and Recreation Department team, her best stroke was the freestyle. She also mastered the backstroke and the breaststroke. "The biggest challenge for me was the butterfly," she said while attending Holyoke Community College in 1994 following her graduation from Agawam High.

That was understandable, since in the butterfly, the leg motion is extremely important. Yet, incredibly, Nancy Bazanchuk, both because of sheer determination and practice, was able to compete in the butterfly by her junior year. "A lot of people, I guess, thought I'd never be able to do the 'fly,'" she said. "I even had my doubts for a while, but I was determined to do it."

Dennis Walters had legs, but lost the use of them on July 21, 1974, when he was trying to qualify for the P.G.A. tour. Only two years out of North Texas State University, which he had attended on a golf scholarship, Walters had spent the 1973 season playing on the South African tour along with tournaments in the U.S. By then, he had already finished eleventh in the U.S. Amateur. Dennis Walters definitely was a hot prospect for the P.G.A. tour.

A short time before the P.G.A. qualifying event in 1974, Walters went home to Neptune, New Jersey, for a visit and to play some golf with friends. As he was driving a golf cart down a fairly steep hill, the brakes failed and the three-wheel cart flipped over, throwing Walters out. He felt no pain and there weren't even any bruises. As it turned out, one of his vertebrae was dislocated and he had suffered severe spinal cord damage. At the age of twenty-four, Dennis Walters was paralyzed from the waist down.

After five months in a hospital, Walters went home determined to find some way to play golf again, even though he could no longer walk. He tried hitting a golf ball from his wheelchair, but that didn't work. One day, while sitting in a clubhouse on a bar stool, an idea struck home: *Why not install a swiveling seat like a bar stool on a golf cart?* Sure, he couldn't take the cart onto a green or into a sand trap, but he could hit those shots with one hand while using his crutches.

The scheme worked. Before long, while ensconced in his swivel seat on a customized golf cart, Walters was hitting the ball beautifully. Maybe not as far as in the past, but far enough and down the middle. He could hit every shot in the book, and soon, he was breaking eighty again.

Walters also began to develop a variety of trick shots, although he preferred to call them "unusual" shots. Other golfers, along with a lot of non-golfers, loved to watch. Before long Walters began giving clinics, out of which evolved "The Dennis Walters Golf Show," which included a remarkable array of "unusual" shots hit from tees as high as three feet with clubs made from everything from crutches to fishing rods to baseball bats. Every shot, though, is hit with precision and accuracy, including a 225-yard drive down the middle while blindfolded.

Traveling with his father, Bucky, Dennis has traveled the country with his mixture of instructional tips, trick shots, and motivational speaking, making about eighty-five appearances a year, while performing his show in conjunction with the P.G.A. "Dennis has demonstrated a tremendous desire to overcome incredible odds, and we're proud to have him associated with the P.G.A.," the organization's executive director, Jim Awtrey, has said.

Even though he was never able to return to the pro golf tour, Walters was made an honorary lifetime member of the P.G.A., joining an elite group that included former President Gerald Ford and Bob Hope. In recognition of his comeback, he won the highly-coveted Ben Hogan Award, given by the Golf Writers of America. Previous recipients have included Babe Didrikson Zaharias, Lee Trevino, Gene Littler, and Fuzzy Zoeller.

"I love what I do, and I'm so glad I was able to stay involved in golf," Walters said during the winter of 1994, as he prepared to fly to Hawaii to put on exhibitions. "And I think I've proven that if there is something you really want to do, no matter how impossible it may seem, with enough hard work and perseverance you can do it."

Because of his talent and hard work, and in spite of his disability, Dennis Walters has become successful and a celebrity of sorts. But most athletes who overcome various handicaps or disabilities to succeed in sports receive little, if any, attention. Not many people outside of Connecticut, for example, have heard about Harry "Lime" Katzman, who in his sixties was still playing two-on-two basketball at the Ansonia, Connecticut, Y.M.C.A.—with one arm—and playing it very well. Katzman, who lost his right arm in an accident at the age of five, kept playing basketball, along with racquetball, well after retiring as the sports editor of the *Evening Sentinel* in Ansonia. In his prime, Katzman was so good with one arm that he played on a semipro team that included seven-foot two-inch Bill Spivey, an All-American at Kentucky in the 1960s.

Amazing? Yes. Then how about Sarah Reinertsen as a one-legged sprinter on the Huntington, New York High School girls' track team in the early 1990s, capable of running the one-hundred-yard dash in eighteen seconds and doing two hundred yards in thirty-seven seconds. As a sprinter Sarah also competed in the four-by-two-hundred-yard relay, wherein four runners each do two hundred yards. And she was no also-ran. "In the individual races, she was usually in the middle of the pack," her coach, Chris Nugent, said. "Most of the opposing runners didn't realize Sarah ran with a prosthesis. And sometimes when I'd tell them or their coaches, they'd say, 'You're lying.' Then I'd bring over Sarah, who was glad to show them her artificial leg."

Earlier, in junior high school, Reinertsen had played doubles on the tennis team and before that, was a soccer player. Later, she excelled in regional, national, and international competition for disabled athletes and participated in the 1992 Paralympics in Barcelona. In 1990, Sarah became the first disabled athlete inducted into the Suffolk County Sports Hall of Fame.

Like many other disabled athletes, Reinertsen's talents extended beyond the playing fields and track ovals. While still in high school, and later at George Washington University, she spoke to numerous groups in an effort to make people more aware of the disabled and some of the marvelous things they can do in sports.

The lack of a leg, in her case one that was lost to cancer when she was five, did not keep Sarah Billmeier of Yarmouth, Maine, from becoming an outstanding skier. Taking up skiing when she was eight, Sarah became one of the world's best disabled skiers, winning three gold medals at the 1992 Paralympics in Albertville, France, when she was only fourteen years old. Then she captured two gold medals and a silver medal during the 1994 Paralympics in Lillehammer, Norway. A good all-round athlete, she also played goalie in both soccer and lacrosse in high school.

Then there are athletes like Foster Anderson who have never competed on the national or international level, but who have thoroughly involved themselves in sports for the sheer love of it all along with the challenge.

As a teenager in Rochester, New York, Anderson was an avid skier, played hockey, and became an expert in the art of throwing and catching a Frisbee. But while riding along an abandoned railroad track when he was seventeen, his motorcycle struck a railroad tie, sending him flying. In a trice, Foster Anderson had gone from an ardent athlete to a quadriplegic.

Determined to carry on the best that he could and pursue his love of the outdoors, Anderson got a degree from the Rochester Institute of Technology, where he majored in manufacturing engineering. Ten years after his accident, Anderson, looking for a new horizon and a new way of life, drove cross country with a friend in his specially equipped van to the San Francisco Bay area. Besides teaching and working as a computer graphics engineer, among other jobs, he started what he would later refer to as his "second life." This included scuba-diving, surfing while lying prone on a surfboard, kayaking, and even bungee-jumping.

A thrill seeker, trying to prove something? "Not at all," Anderson said during an interview from his Santa Cruz, California, home in the spring of 1994. "I just like to stay active and do things."

Bent on helping other quadriplegics, Anderson, who has no movement in his fingers, has invented, patented, and marketed a "Quad Disc," a Frisbee-like device that can be gripped by people with little if any, finger movement. Relying on his engineering background and his own paralysis, he also invented the "Super Spat," a lightweight spatula designed for people with arthritis or, like himself, with spinal injuries.

"I think I'm living a pretty full life," he said.

More so, it would seem, than many, if indeed, not most able-bodied people.

For far too long, disabled athletes have been either largely ignored or, when they've drawn attention at all, viewed as some kind of sports sideshow akin to a tent circus act. In some instances, such as at major marathon races, wheelchair racers have even been perceived as a nuisance, even though they set off and finish well before the able-bodied runners. Fortunately, such a view is no longer widely shared, thanks in part to the proliferation of sports involving disabled athletes. Since the 1980s, they have also received greater media attention.

Above all, the vast majority of disabled athletes would no doubt like to be regarded as, first and foremost, "athletes," which they are—some so good that they even have agents, a sign in itself of acceptance. Once he established himself as a big league pitcher, no one called Jim Abbott a "disabled pitcher." The same thing was true, to a lesser extent, of Pete Gray when he made it to the major leagues as a one-armed outfielder. Unfortunately, sportswriters in a less enlightened era when it came to physical disabilities, dubbed Gray "The One-Armed Wonder," a term he abhorred. The term helped embitter Gray and convince him that people looked at him as a freak and not a legitimate baseball player, a view he still held almost a half-century after he played in the big leagues. "They thought I was a freak," he told me during an interview in the mid-1980s, "but I was a good ballplayer."

Like Jim Abbott with one hand, Pete Gray, with one arm, was indeed a good ballplayer. I tried my best to convince him that's what counted, and that most people who got to watch him play realized it and admired him for his wondrous accomplishments in the face of his disability, but it was too late. Pete Gray had spent almost a lifetime convinced that baseball fans had perceived him as a freak. He was not about to change his opinion. Deep down, though, he knew he had been a good ballplayer; yet he remained resentful.

Apart from Abbott few, if any, disabled athletes will achieve the celebrity, brief though it was, of Pete Gray; but that's not why they get involved, or re-involved, in sports in the first place. Mainly they do so for the pure love of the sport, or in Dawn Storrs' case, her love of dancing. They do so because of the competition and the camaraderie it can engender, or because they want to stay as active as possible and lead a full and healthy life.

They do not want sympathy, nor do they want to be patronized. What they want is what they deserve—to be accepted as athletes who also play the game.